TO: ....

FROM: ....

Editorial Director: Delia Berrigan
Editor: Emily Osborn
Art Director: Chris Opheim
Designer: Mark Voss
Production Designer: Dan Horton

ISBN: 978-1-59530-559-6
SKU: XKT1310

Printed and bound in China

CHRISTMAS COOKIES

• A COLLECTION OF VERY MERRY HOLIDAY RECIPES •

A SHORT HISTORY OF CHRISTMAS COOKIES

Since medieval times, Christmas cookies have been a tradition in northern and central Europe, particularly Scandinavia, Holland, and Germany. Many of these cookies are formed by using carved wooden molds to stamp out fruits, animals, human figures, or hearts.

German Lebkuchen, honey spice cookies that are the ancestor of gingerbread, are typically made in the shape of a heart or of Saint Nicholas. They are sold today in German villages at street fairs and in big city markets from the beginning of Advent until Christmas. Germany's anise-scented Springerle date back to midwinter festivals at which animals were sacrificed to the gods, but because the poor could not afford to butcher their animals, they offered baked tokens in the form of animal cookies. Many of these offerings took the shape of a rearing steed, as the word Springerle derives from the German phrase for "a vaulting horse." Town bakers were frequently responsible for the beautiful early molds that we now see in museums. The shop with the prettiest cookies was likely to capture the biggest holiday trade.

Until the Middle Ages, adding spices to cookie dough was uncommon, however. Spices were rare and costly, affordable only by the wealthy, a situation that prompted bakers to use ginger and pepper interchangeably. This fact explains why so many Christmastime and year-round ginger cookies have a pepper prefix, even though they lack that spice as an ingredient. Swedish pepparkakor and German Pfeffernüsse are examples.

In Holland, the early molds for speculaas, a spice cookie, depicted holiday scenes or events. These popular cookies were also favored as a way of delivering announcements or messages, by stamping words into the cookies before they were slipped into the oven.

Farther north, in Scotland, shortbread has long been a traditional Christmas and New Year's treat. The rich butter cake descends from the oatmeal bannock served at pagan Yule celebrations. The round bannock was scored in the center with a circle surrounded by wedges. This was meant to symbolize the sun and its rays. Because it was considered unlucky to cut the shortbread into portions, it was always broken into pieces by hand.

For centuries, spritz cookies, beloved in Sweden and Denmark, have been extruded from cookie presses into rounds, wreaths, and S's. Emigrants from these countries quickly popularized the buttery cookies when they settled in new homes in America.

Some version of peppernuts, spicy morsels the size of a nut, can be found in a handful of European countries. In Holland they are pepernoten, in Denmark pebernodder, and in Germany Pfeffernüsse. Creating them was a community affair: the dough was mixed and left to mellow in crocks for months, then rolled out in assembly-line fashion, baked, and stored in jars until Christmas, when they would be eaten.

In Italy, cookies have mainly been the domain of the pasticcerie, or pastry shops, and home cooks simply bought their cookies. The almond paste cookies that are favorites throughout the country probably stem from the marzipan of Sicily that arrived with the Arabs. They also introduced cane sugar, almonds, and spices to the island. Nuns in the local convents perfected the recipes, adorning the cookies with angels and fondant frostings that resembled cathedral ceilings, and kept how to make them secret. In France as well, cookies were—and continue to be—the provenance of the professional baker, and the French traditionally visit their favorite pastry shops at holiday time, stocking up on delicate buttery cookies carefully packed in ribbon-bound boxes.

Today during the holiday season, families in many cultures bake and pass along their treasured family Christmas cookies, looking upon them as cherished heirlooms from past generations. This practice of sharing festive sweets made from traditional recipes is a wonderful way to renew old friendships and launch new ones.

THE BASICS

ingredients

High-quality ingredients are essential to turning out batches of the best cookies possible. To ensure that every cookie you bake has the finest flavor, always store ingredients properly and never use ingredients that are past their prime. The following annotated list includes pantry staples used in this book.

baking powder and baking soda

Baking powder and baking soda are both leavening agents, but they cannot be used interchangeably. Baking soda is only used in dough that contains an acid, such as brown sugar, yogurt, lemon juice, or molasses, to activate it. Baking powder must be stored airtight in a cool, dark place and used within 6 months, as it easily loses its leavening power. Stale baking powder may also leave an unpleasant aftertaste. Baking soda is not as perishable, but you should still update your supply once a year.

butter

Unsalted butter is preferred for making cookies, as it has a more delicate, fresher flavor than salted butter. A package labeled with the term sweet cream butter is misleading, as this is actually salted butter. The recipes were tested with unsalted butter, so if you use salted butter, you may want to reduce the salt called for in a recipe. While unsalted butter has a shorter refrigerator shelf life than salted butter, it keeps well in the freezer for up to 6 months.

chocolate and unsweetened cocoa powder

Chocolate products vary in amounts of sugar, cocoa butter, and chocolate liquor. Bittersweet and semisweet chocolate are similar, as both are sweetened, but bittersweet, which generally contains more chocolate liquor, often imparts a smoother, richer flavor. It is also usually less sweet than semisweet. Sometimes the two are interchangeable. Unsweetened chocolate is chocolate liquor and cocoa butter and it tastes quite bitter. Always purchase high-quality domestic or imported chocolate for the best baking results.

Unsweetened cocoa powder is made from the hardened cocoa liquor that remains after the making of chocolate. This solid mass is dried and ground to produce the powder. The richer Dutch-process cocoa powder has been treated to neutralize the natural acidity of cocoa.

eggs

All the recipes were tested with large eggs. If a recipe calls for separating the yolks and whites, make certain that the whites contain no egg yolk, as even a trace of yolk contains fat that prevents proper beating. If uncooked egg whites are specified in an icing and egg safety is a concern, use pasteurized egg whites.

flours

All-purpose flour, either bleached or unbleached, can be used in these recipes. This is a fine-textured flour that contains neither the germ nor the bran. Whole-wheat flour, which contains the wheat germ and natural bran of the grain, adds a fuller flavor and higher fiber content.

Nut flours, including almond, hazelnut (filbert), pecan, walnut, and pistachio, lend a wonderful flavor to many doughs.

nuts

Fresh top-quality nuts are essential. Refrigerate nuts for up to 2 months, or if you don't intend to use them within a short time, freeze them for up to 1 year. Longer storage results in diminished flavor. When a recipe calls for grinding nuts, it is smart to add a tablespoon of sugar to prevent the nuts from becoming an oily paste.

Toasting nuts helps bring out their flavor. Hazelnuts (filberts), however, are toasted not only to intensify their flavor, but also to remove their skins. Instructions for toasting all nuts are given below, under making & storing cookies. Sometimes one nut can be substituted for another. Use your own judgment, taking into consideration similar textures. Almonds and hazelnuts or walnuts and pecans are often interchangeable. With their green color, pistachios add a holiday look and can often substitute for walnuts.

Almond paste is a dense, stiff mixture of ground blanched almonds, sugar, and a syrupy liquid. It is available in 6 to 8-ounce cans and packages.

spices and flavorings

Purchase spices in stores that have a good turnover in stock, and store the spices in airtight containers in a cool pantry. Spices deteriorate in flavor after a year and can develop a musty flavor, so if you have kept them too long, discard them and buy a new supply. When vanilla or almond extract is called for, use a pure extract rather than an imitation or artificial one.

sweeteners

When simply sugar is specified in a recipe, use granulated sugar. Brown sugar comes in both light and dark styles, the dark being slightly stronger in flavor because it contains a bit more molasses. The brown sugars generally can be used interchangeably and should nearly always be firmly packed for the correct measure. If your brown sugar hardens, place a slice of apple in the container and it should soften within a day.

Powdered sugar, also known as confectioners' sugar, is granulated sugar that has been crushed to a fine powder. To prevent caking, it is mixed with about 3 percent cornstarch. Unless a recipe specifies sifting, it is not necessary to sift powdered sugar before using it. One cup of granulated sugar is equivalent to 1 3⁄4 cups (packed) powdered sugar.

Natural, unrefined, or milled brown sugars include honey-colored and large-grained demerara and turbinado, as well as the fine-grained, richly flavored light and dark muscovados, which are suitable for baking. The latter come from the island of Mauritius, off the coast of Africa, and only recently have become available in the United States.

Also in the marketplace are eye-catching decorating sugars in a broad spectrum of colors. Shapes vary from rounds to confetti to stamped-out designs. Some are sparkling. They are ideal for giving a Christmas spin to baked goods. Sources are listed on page 93.

Honey provides a fragrance and flavor depending on the flower nectar the bees visited. In general, the darker the color, the stronger the flavor. Orange blossom, clover, and sage are popular mild honeys.

Molasses, which comes in light and dark forms and is a by-product of sugar making, adds a robust flavor and rich color to baked goods. Unsulfured molasses, produced when no sulfur is used in the refining process, is preferred for its flavor, as sulfured molasses often carries a light sulfur taste.

baking sheets

Well-made, clean baking sheets are essential to cookie success. Medium-weight aluminum sheets with just one or two narrow rims work well. (The absence of rims on two or three sides makes removing cookies easier.) Sheets that are dark or have blackened undersides disrupt the normal browning process. Nonstick cushioned sheets with a medium-light gray, rather than black, surface work well. It is useful to have at least two baking sheets.

measuring cups and spoons

Be sure to use the proper cups for measuring dry and wet ingredients. Cups for dry measures usually come in a graduated set from 1⁄4 cup to 1 cup (sometimes 1⁄8 cup is included), are made out of stainless steel or sturdy plastic, and have an even rim. Cups for liquid measures are typically clear glass or plastic, have vertical markings for fluid ounces and cups on the side, and include a pour spout. A set of measuring spoons, which are suitable for wet and dry measures, is also needed.

electric mixer

Most cookie doughs may be mixed by hand, but a handheld electric mixer is a great aid, especially for crumbly crusts for bar cookies, and an electric stand mixer is needed for doughs that require a wire whip for mixing.

food processor and blender

Some shortbread-type doughs and bar-cookie crusts work best if prepared in a food processor or with an electric mixer, due to the need for a crumbly consistency. Nuts and chocolate may be chopped by hand, but a blender or a food processor is handy for grinding them finely. It is a good idea to add 1 tablespoon of sugar to nuts when grinding them to prevent overprocessing, which results in an oily paste.

pastry bag

Although not necessary, a pastry bag is nice to have for adding icing decorations to cookies. Choose one with a variety of tips for the maximum versatility.

rack

A wire rack for cooling lets air circulate, so that the cookies cool evenly. Have a few in your cupboard for handling big cookie batches.

spatulas and cookie cutters

A thin-bladed, flexible spatula is essential for transferring cookies. A small icing spatula is ideal for decorating freshly baked cookies. A rubber spatula or plastic pastry scraper is useful for scraping dough from a bowl, while a rubber spatula is also ideal for doughs that require the folding in of ingredients and for cleaning down the sides of a blender or food processor. Cutters may be of any design or holiday motif you choose. Metal cutters give the best edge.

MAKING & STORING COOKIES

before you begin

Read the recipe all the way through before you take a mixing bowl or measuring cup off the shelf. Then, preheat the oven as the first step, unless the dough is mixed and chilled before shaping. Allow at least 15 minutes for the oven to reach the correct temperature. If you have an oven thermometer, use it to check that your oven is heating to the temperature you have indicated. If it is not, adjust the temperature as needed. For example, if the oven control is set at 350°F and the oven heats only to 325°F, then reset the control to 375°F.

assembling and measuring the ingredients

Get out all of the ingredients you will need for the recipe. The exceptions are those that must be added chilled, such as butter when making crumbly doughs. Measure each ingredient accurately using the proper measuring cups for dry and wet ingredients. Measure flour unsifted, using the sweep-and-level method: dip the appropriate cup or spoon into the flour until heaping, then level off with a straight-edged metal spatula or a table knife blade. Measure dry ingredients in tablespoons and teaspoons by overfilling the standard measuring spoons and leveling the top with the straight edge of a metal spatula or a table knife.

mixing and beating

Most cookie recipes call for a minimum of mixing. A food processor or electric mixer is desirable for bar-cookie crusts and shortbread-style cookies, to create the necessary crumbly consistency. A large spoon is sufficient for mixing many of the doughs, but an electric mixer makes mixing stiff doughs easier, and a stand mixer is indispensable when a whip attachment is indicated. Sifting the dry ingredients for the recipes in this book is not necessary, but it is important to stir them together thoroughly to distribute the leavening and spices evenly before you begin mixing in other ingredients.

rolling out the dough

Use as little flour as possible on the work surface when rolling out cookie dough. Most dough needs to be chilled for at least 1 to 2 hours to firm up before rolling. To speed up the process, some doughs may be frozen for 30 to 40 minutes. Many professional pastry chefs roll out the dough between sheets of waxed paper, chill the rolled-out sheets still in the paper, and then peel off the paper and cut out the cookies. If you find this tedious, as I do, skip the waxed paper. Sometimes it is useful to lay a sheet of waxed paper on the dough before you roll it out, especially if it is a soft dough. You can reroll scraps once. Pat them together and chill them again if they have warmed too much. Rerolling them more than once may result in tough cookies.

toasting nuts

For many recipes, the flavor of nuts is enhanced by toasting them in the oven before mixing them into the dough. Place them in a baking pan and bake in a preheated 325°F oven for 8 to 10 minutes, or until light brown (pine nuts need only 6 to 8 minutes). To skin hazelnuts, let the toasted nuts cool for 1 to 2 minutes, then rub the still-warm nuts between the palms of your hands, layers of a kitchen towel, or paper towels, letting the papery skins flake away. It is not necessary to remove every bit of skin.

spacing cookies for baking

Allow ample space between the cookies to allow for spreading during baking. Some cookies, such as Almond Tiles (page 86) and Florentines (page 76), spread more than other cookies. Each recipe specifies the proper spacing.

baking

Allow at least 2 inches of space around each baking sheet in the oven, so that the hot air can circulate freely. In some ovens, you may need to rotate the pan 180 degrees halfway through baking for the cookies to brown evenly. Bake only one sheet of cookies at a time for even browning.

checking for doneness

Check the cookies at least 2 minutes before the time specified for baking them, using the visual cue that is included in each recipe to judge for doneness.

cooling

Cookies should be cooled on the baking sheet until firm enough to be transferred to a rack without breaking. This usually takes just a minute or two. Lace cookies are ideally baked on aluminum foil, as the foil can be slipped off of the baking sheet onto a countertop and the cookies left to cool, at which point the cookies will peel right off. Do not use parchment paper for lace cookies. It prevents them from spreading.

storing

Airtight containers should be used for storing all cookies. It is best to store just one kind of cookie in each container. Frosted cookies should be layered with waxed paper between the layers. Cookies vary in how long they stay fresh at room temperature. Most cookies stay fresh several days at room temperature. Lemon bars are an exception, as they are best within a day or two and should be refrigerated. Frosted cookies and rich chocolate cookies do not keep as long at room temperature as unfrosted, plain cookies. Freeze the cookies if they are not served within 2 or 3 days, as it better preserves a just-baked flavor. Biscotti and Springerle are excellent keepers in an airtight container at room temperature and do not benefit from freezing. If necessary, biscotti gain a fresh-baked flavor with rebaking in a 300°F oven for 10 minutes. Each recipe includes a suggested storing time, but you might consider freezing the cookies after 2 or 3 days. Store at room temperature, unless otherwise indicated.

Most cookies, with the exception of biscotti, freeze well. Put them in heavy-duty freezer bags, expelling as much air as possible, or pack them in airtight containers. Bar cookies can be frozen whole before cutting. Slip the baked sheet into a freezer bag. As a general rule, cookies may be frozen for 1 to 2 months. They can be thawed at room temperature, unless otherwise indicated.

DECORATING COOKIES

Many cookies are delicious unadorned, but a simple glaze or icing can add a charming and often sophisticated look and a personal artistic touch. The beautiful new decorating sugars in a range of colors and shapes are wonderful for embellishing cutout cookies. Have a selection on hand to add an instant Christmas flair.

Cutout cookies are ideal for icing in a special way. Children and teenagers enjoy giving trees, stars, bells, angels, gingerbread men, and snowmen distinctive personalities. Use the icing to outline the cookies or to add features. The whole family will enjoy giving sugar and spice cutout cookies a holiday profile, a look they only have this season.

A chocolate glaze adds a special touch to biscotti, or it can be used to form a half-moon design on a round cookie, a filling for a sandwich cookie, or a fanciful drizzle on a cookie of any shape or size. You can dip the end of a cookie bar in chocolate and leave it plain, or immediately dip it into multicolored or silver sprinkles. A shower of powdered sugar—vanilla flavored or plain—gives the simplest cookie a wonderful wintry look.

PRESENTING COOKIE PLATTERS

In planning cookie platters or plates for a party, consider serving at least four or five kinds of cookies. Offer a variety of contrasting shapes, flavors, colors, and textures. Or for a large party, use a different plate for serving each batch of cookies.

Use your imagination to create eye-catching presentations. Arrange the cookies on an antique silver tray or gold-rimmed platters for an elegant occasion, or stack them in a large Chinese basket threaded with red ribbon and decorated with red and silver glass ornaments for a more casual affair. A beautiful holiday box, outfitted with a big, shiny silk bow and a cluster of silver stars and with its lid to one side, makes a handsome container.

Array cookies on plain white platters and surround them with colorful edible flowers, herb wreaths of blue-green rosemary or dense green bay, boughs of holly, or a scattering of dried pine cones. Put together a centerpiece of winter's favorite citrus fruits—oranges, lemons, mandarins, limes, kumquats—and ring it with shortbread and/or biscotti. Or place clear glass platters of cookies atop a sea of deep red rose petals.

A cookie exchange is a great informal way to show off your baking efforts and to discover new cookies at the same time. Contact four or five friends who also love to bake at Christmastime and have them each bake a batch of five dozen cookies. Set the ground rules beforehand, checking on the flavors and types so that the same kind is not duplicated. If five friends each bring five dozen cookies, each person will go home with a dozen each of five different kinds of cookies—and some new holiday recipes.

GIFT WRAPPING COOKIES

Hand delivering cookies to neighbors and friends is a thoughtful custom. Containers can range from a festive paper plate to an antique cookie tin. Other possibilities include fancy clear glass jars, small hatboxes, old-fashioned cigar boxes, pretty bakery boxes, baskets in all sizes and shapes, glass or pottery plates or bowls, or old-fashioned plain round cookie tins dressed up with ribbon and perhaps an ornament for the holiday tree. Also consider new or recycled springform pans, wooden cutting boards, widemouthed glass containers and, of course, new or even secondhand cookie jars found at a great garage sale or next-to-new shop. It is sometimes nice to tie a cookie cutter and the recipe onto the package.

Utilize colored cellophane for wrapping a festive paper plate. Or pick up a lovely embossed glass plate on a sale table. Gift bags are ideal for sturdy cookies such as biscotti, if you first pack them in a resealable plastic bag. Festoon your cookie gift with satin ribbon, rustic raffia, or metallic twine, and attach a gift tag with a note from your kitchen. Or cut out images from old Christmas cards and paste them on card stock to use for gift tags. Recipes are always welcome, lettered by hand or printed on a card.

BOXING COOKIES FOR MAILING

The best cookies for mailing are nonfragile ones that keep well. Bar cookies are ideal for wrapping in foil and packaging stacked in layers. Fairly sturdy drop cookies can be stacked to form a cylinder and wrapped in plastic wrap. Place the cylinder or layered bar cookies in a gift container, then put the container in a heavy-duty, corrugated box. The box should be larger than the package of cookies to allow room for packing materials, such as bubble wrap, popcorn, newspaper, crumpled paper, or Styrofoam peanuts. It is a good idea to put those fly-away peanuts in plastic bags to tame them, then use the resulting pillows as cushions. Tape the box securely closed, address it clearly, and carry it to your favorite overnight or two-day mailing service.

THUMBPRINTS

MAKES
3 1/2
DOZEN

These cookies get their name from the fact that you use your thumb to make an indentation into each ball of dough and then fill it with jam. For variety, roll the balls in chopped nuts or dried coconut before making the indentation.

Ingredients:

2/3 cup sugar
1 cup (2 sticks) butter,
(at room temperature)
1/2 teaspoon almond extract
1/2 teaspoon vanilla extract
2 cups plus 3 tablespoons flour
1/3 cup raspberry jam

Directions:

1. Preheat oven to 350°F.
2. In a large bowl, with an electric mixer, combine the sugar, butter, almond and vanilla extracts. Beat at medium speed until creamy, 1 to 2 minutes.
3. Reduce speed to low and add the flour. Continue beating until well mixed.
4. Take a scoop of dough about the size of a small walnut and roll into a smooth ball.
5. Place the balls 2 inches apart on baking sheets.
6. With your thumb, make an indentation in the center and fill each thumbprint with about 1/4 teaspoon jam.
7. Bake for 15 minutes until light brown around the bottom edges, but pale on top.
8. Allow to cool on the baking sheets for 1 minute; then transfer to wire racks to cool completely.

Different Spins:

1. Glazed Thumbprints:
   Make a sugar glaze by sifting together 3/4 cup confectioners' sugar, 1 teaspoon almond extract, and 2 to 3 teaspoons water (enough to make a thin glaze).
   Drizzle the glaze over the cooled cookies.

2. Chocolate Thumbprints:
   Omit the jam and fill the thumbprint in each cookie with about 1/2 teaspoon mini chocolate chips (2/3 cup total).

KOURABIEDES

MAKES
3
DOZEN

Shaped in rounds and half-moons, these greek butter-cookies are an integral part of any family's holidays. At Christmastime, it is typical to imbed a whole clove in the center of each to signify the spices brought by the Magi to the Christ child.

Ingredients:

1 cup unsalted butter,
(at room temperature)
3 tablespoons powdered sugar
1 egg yolk
1/2 teaspoon almond extract
1/8 teaspoon salt
2 cups all-purpose flour
2/3 cup ground lightly toasted,
blanched almonds (page 15)
About 36 whole cloves
Powdered sugar for coating

Directions:

1. Preheat the oven to 325°F.
2. Lightly grease baking sheets, or use nonstick or parchment-lined baking sheets. Alternatively, use nonstick baking sheets.
3. In a bowl, using an electric mixer or a spoon, cream together the butter, powdered sugar, and egg yolk until light and fluffy.
4. Add the almond extract, salt, flour, and nuts and mix until well blended.
5. Roll the dough into small 3/4-inch balls or 1 3/4-inch-long crescents with tapered ends, inserting a clove into the center of each one.
6. Place on the prepared baking sheets, spacing them about 1 1/2 inches apart.
7. One sheet at a time, bake the cookies for 15 to 18 minutes, or until lightly browned. Transfer to racks to cool slightly.
8. Shake powdered sugar through a sieve onto a sheet of parchment paper or aluminum foil, making a 3/8-inch-thick coating. Carefully lay the warm cookies atop the sugar and continue dusting them with sugar until they are coated with a layer about 3/8 inch thick. Let cool completely.

SWISS HAZELNUT HALF-MOONS

The subtle scent of cloves and cinnamon permeates these delicate ground hazelnut rounds.

MAKES
5
DOZEN

Ingredients:

1 vanilla bean
3⁄4 cup plus 2 tablespoons
unsalted butter,
(at room temperature)
1 cup firmly packed light brown sugar
1⁄8 teaspoon salt
3⁄4 teaspoon ground cinnamon
1⁄2 teaspoon ground cloves
1 egg yolk
2 tablespoons milk
1 cup ground lightly toasted,
skinned hazelnuts (page 15)
1 1⁄2 cups all-purpose flour

CHOCOLATE GLAZE:
3 ounces bittersweet chocolate
1 ounce unsweetened chocolate
1⁄4 teaspoon vegetable shortening

Directions:

PART 1:

1. Split the vanilla bean lengthwise and, using the tip of a knife, scrape the seeds into a bowl.
2. Add the butter, brown sugar, salt, cinnamon, and cloves and, using an electric mixer or a spoon, cream together until blended.
3. Mix in the egg yolk and milk, then add the hazelnuts and flour and mix until blended.
4. On a sheet of plastic wrap, using the wrap, not your fingers, shape half of the dough into a log about 2 inches in diameter. Repeat with the remaining dough.
5. Wrap each log and chill for 1 hour, or until firm.

PART 2:

1. Preheat the oven to 375°F.
2. Line baking sheets with parchment paper.
3. Slice the logs into rounds 3⁄16 inch thick and place on the prepared baking sheets, spacing them about 1 inch apart.
4. Bake the cookies for 8 to 10 minutes, or until golden brown. Transfer to racks to cool.

PART 3:

1. To make the glaze, combine the chocolates and shortening in the top pan of a double boiler.
2. Place over hot water and heat until melted, then stir until smooth.
3. Using an icing spatula, spread half of each cookie with the glaze. Chill until set.

GINGERBREAD

MAKES
8
DOZEN

This is the perfect place to have fun with the newly marketed decorating sugars—sparkling ones, little balls, confetti, and decorative designs. Use the sugars to decorate wreaths with red holly berries, trees with ornaments, santas with buttons and beards, and bells with silvery dragées.

Ingredients:

1/2 cup unsalted butter,
(at room temperature)
1/2 cup sugar
1 egg
1/2 cup dark molasses
1 tablespoon cider vinegar
3 cups all-purpose flour
3/4 teaspoon baking soda
1/4 teaspoon salt
2 teaspoons ground ginger
1/2 teaspoon ground cinnamon

VANILLA BUTTER ICING:
2 tablespoons unsalted butter,
(at room temperature)
2 cups sifted powdered sugar
1 teaspoon vanilla extract
4 to 6 tablespoons water

Red cinnamon candies, green sugar,
and silver dragées for decorating

Directions:

1. In a bowl, using an electric mixer or a spoon, cream together the butter and sugar until light.
2. Mix in the egg, molasses, and vinegar, beating until smooth.
3. In another bowl, stir together the flour, baking soda, salt, ginger, and cinnamon.
4. Add the flour mixture to the egg mixture and mix just until blended.
5. Scrape the dough onto a sheet of plastic wrap and flatten into a disk.
6. Wrap and chill for 2 hours, or until firm.
7. Preheat the oven to 375°F.
8. Lightly grease baking sheets, or use nonstick or parchment-lined baking sheets.
9. On a lightly floured surface, roll out the dough 1/8 inch thick.
10. Cut out with 1 1/2- to 2-inch decorative cutters of choice. Or use larger cutters for gingerbread people.
11. Place on prepared baking sheets, spacing them about 1 inch apart.
12. One sheet at a time, bake the cookies for 6 to 8 minutes, or until light brown on the edges.
13. Transfer to racks to cool.

FOR THE ICING:

1. In a bowl, beat together the butter, powdered sugar, and vanilla, then beat in enough of the water to make a spreading consistency.
2. Spread the icing on the cooled cookies, or spoon it into a pastry bag fitted with a fine tip and pipe it decoratively onto the cookies.
3. Immediately decorate with the candies, green sugar, and dragées, then let the cookies stand until the icing is set.

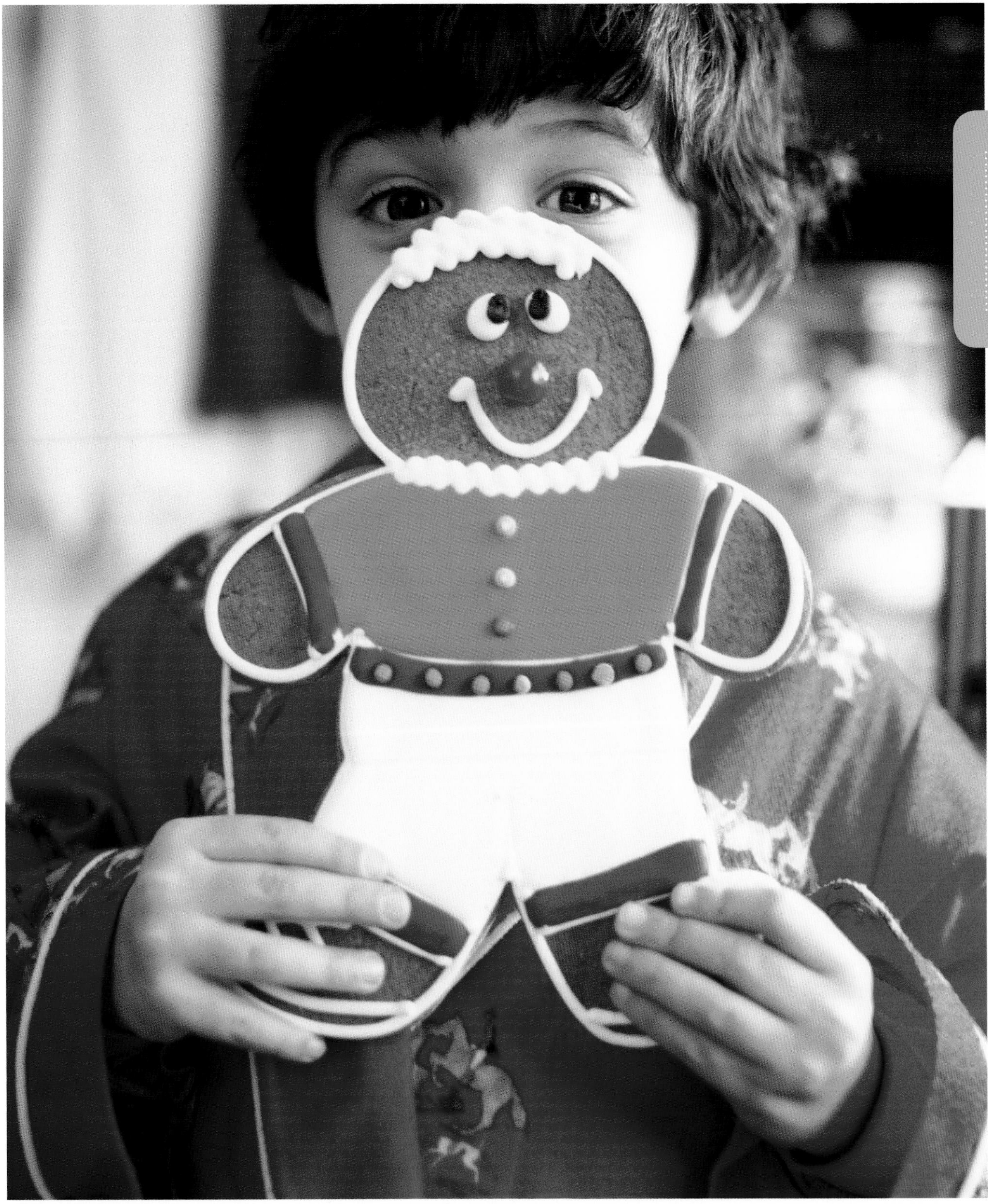

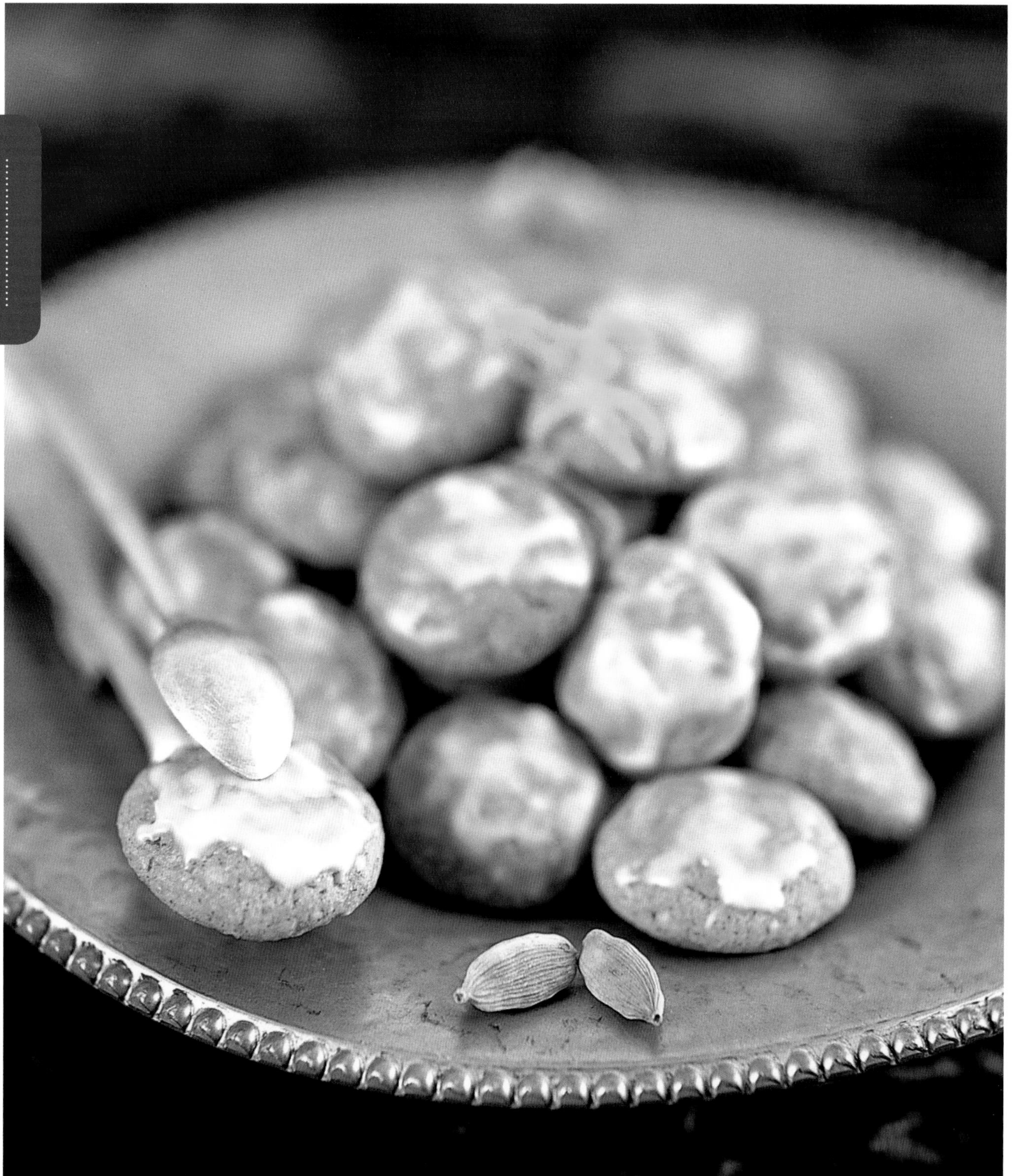

PEPPERNUTS

MAKES
6
DOZEN

Peppernuts, known as pfeffernüsse in Germany, are spicy sweets about the size of a hazelnut, often enlivened with pepper along with an array of other spices. Mennonite families adopted these cookies from the recipes of German, Dutch, and West Prussian bakers.

Ingredients:

1⁄2 cup unsalted butter,
(at room temperature)

1 cup firmly packed dark brown sugar

3 tablespoons honey

1 egg

2 1⁄4 cups all-purpose flour

1 teaspoon baking powder

1⁄2 teaspoon baking soda

1⁄4 teaspoon salt

1 teaspoon ground cinnamon

1 teaspoon ground cardamom

1⁄2 teaspoon ground allspice

1⁄2 teaspoon ground cloves

1⁄4 teaspoon white pepper

1⁄2 cup ground raw almonds or
skinned, toasted hazelnuts (page 15)

COGNAC GLAZE:

1⁄2 cup powdered sugar

2 teaspoons Cognac

Directions:

PART 1:

1. In a large bowl, cream together the butter and brown sugar until light.
2. Beat in the honey and egg until well mixed.
3. In another bowl, stir together the flour, baking powder, baking soda, salt, cinnamon, cardamom, allspice, cloves, white pepper, and nuts. Blend the flour mixture with the butter mixture.
4. Shape into a ball, wrap in plastic wrap, and chill overnight.

PART 2:

1. Preheat the oven to 375°F.
2. Lightly grease baking sheets, or use nonstick or parchment-lined baking sheets.
3. Roll the dough into 3⁄4-inch balls between your palms and place them on the baking sheets, spacing them about 1 inch apart.
4. Bake the cookies for 8 to 10 minutes, or until light brown.
5. Transfer to racks.

FOR THE GLAZE:

1. In a bowl, stir together the powdered sugar and Cognac, adding a few drops of water if necessary.
2. Brush the glaze over the tops of the cookies.
3. Let cool completely.

CHRISTMAS BISCOTTI

MAKES
4
DOZEN

Biscotti are ideal holiday cookies, as they can be made weeks in advance and they keep beautifully without freezing. If they should need to be recrisped, reheat them in a 300°F oven for a few minutes, and once again they will have a fresh-baked flavor. By slicing the baked loaves thinly, the cookies become bite-sized nibbles, which allows guests to sample the whole array of cookies at your holiday party.

Ingredients:

1/2 cup unsalted butter,
(at room temperature)
3/4 cup sugar
2 eggs
1 teaspoon vanilla extract
2 teaspoons grated orange zest
2 1/4 cups all-purpose flour
1 1/2 teaspoons baking powder
1/2 teaspoon ground cloves
1/4 teaspoon salt
1 cup dried cranberries or coarsely
chopped dried cherries
2/3 cup raw pistachio nuts

Directions:

1. Preheat the oven to 325°F.
2. Butter and flour a baking sheet.
3. In a bowl, cream together the butter and sugar until light and fluffy.
4. Beat in the eggs, vanilla, and orange zest until blended.
5. In another bowl, stir together the flour, baking powder, cloves, and salt.
6. Add the flour mixture to the butter mixture and beat until blended.
7. Stir in the cranberries or cherries and nuts.
8. Divide the dough in half.
9. One at a time, place the 2 dough portions on the prepared baking sheet and form each into a log about 1/2 inch high, 1 1/2 inches wide, and 14 inches long. Space the logs at least 2 inches apart.
10. Bake the logs for 25 to 30 minutes, or until set and light brown.
11. Transfer to a cutting board and let cool for 6 to 8 minutes.
12. Reduce the oven temperature to 300°F.
13. Using a serrated knife, cut the logs on the diagonal into slices 3/8 inch thick.
14. Stand the slices upright on the baking sheet and return the sheet to the oven for 15 minutes to dry the cookies thoroughly.
15. Transfer to racks to cool.

PECAN SNOWDROPS

MAKES
3
DOZEN

These rich, sugar-dusted cookies
are timeless classics. For gift giving,
slip them into small foil candy cups
and pack them in an attractive tin
or gift box.

Ingredients:

3⁄4 cup butter,
(at room temperature)
1⁄3 cup powdered sugar
1 teaspoon vanilla extract
1⁄8 teaspoon salt
1 1⁄2 cups all-purpose flour
3⁄4 cup finely chopped pecans or
toasted, skinned hazelnuts (page 15)
Powdered sugar for dusting

Directions:

1. Preheat the oven to 325°F.
2. Lightly grease baking sheets, or use nonstick or parchment-lined
   baking sheets.
3. In a large bowl, using an electric mixer or a spoon, cream together
   the butter and sugar until light and fluffy.
4. Add the vanilla, salt, flour, and nuts and mix well.
5. Roll the dough into 3⁄4-inch balls between your palms, and place on
   the prepared baking sheets, spacing them about 1 1⁄2 inches apart.
6. One sheet at a time, bake the cookies for 15 to 18 minutes,
   or until light brown.
7. Transfer to racks to cool slightly.
8. Place the still-warm cookies on a sheet of parchment paper or
   aluminum foil and heavily dust with powdered sugar shaken
   through a sieve.
9. Let cool completely.

CARDAMOM SHORTBREAD STARS

MAKES
20
COOKIES

Shortbread has been a traditional Christmas treat in Scotland for centuries. The sparkle of freshly ground cardamom, which has a zippy lemon-ginger overtone, punctuates these swift-to-mix cookies.

Ingredients:

1 tablespoon cardamom seeds
1 1/4 cups all-purpose flour
1/3 cup granulated sugar
1/2 cup chilled unsalted butter,
(cut into pieces)
Powdered sugar for dusting

Directions:

1. Place the cardamom seeds in a spice grinder and grind finely.
2. In a food processor or electric mixer, combine the flour, granulated sugar, butter, and ground cardamom.
3. Process or mix until the mixture forms fine crumbs.
4. Pat the dough together and knead it on a lightly floured surface until it forms a ball.
5. Wrap in plastic wrap and chill for 30 minutes, or until firm.
6. Preheat the oven to 350°F. Have ready an ungreased baking sheet.
7. On a lightly floured surface, roll out the dough about 3/16 inch thick.
8. With a 2-inch star cutter, cut out the cookies and transfer to a baking sheet, spacing them about 1 inch apart.
9. Bake the cookies for 12 to 15 minutes, or until the bottoms are golden.
10. Transfer to racks and let cool slightly.
11. While the cookies are still barely warm, dust the tops with powdered sugar shaken through a sieve.
12. Let cool completely.

VARIATION:
Omit the cardamom and use in its place a 1/2 teaspoon vanilla seeds, scraped from a vanilla bean split lengthwise.

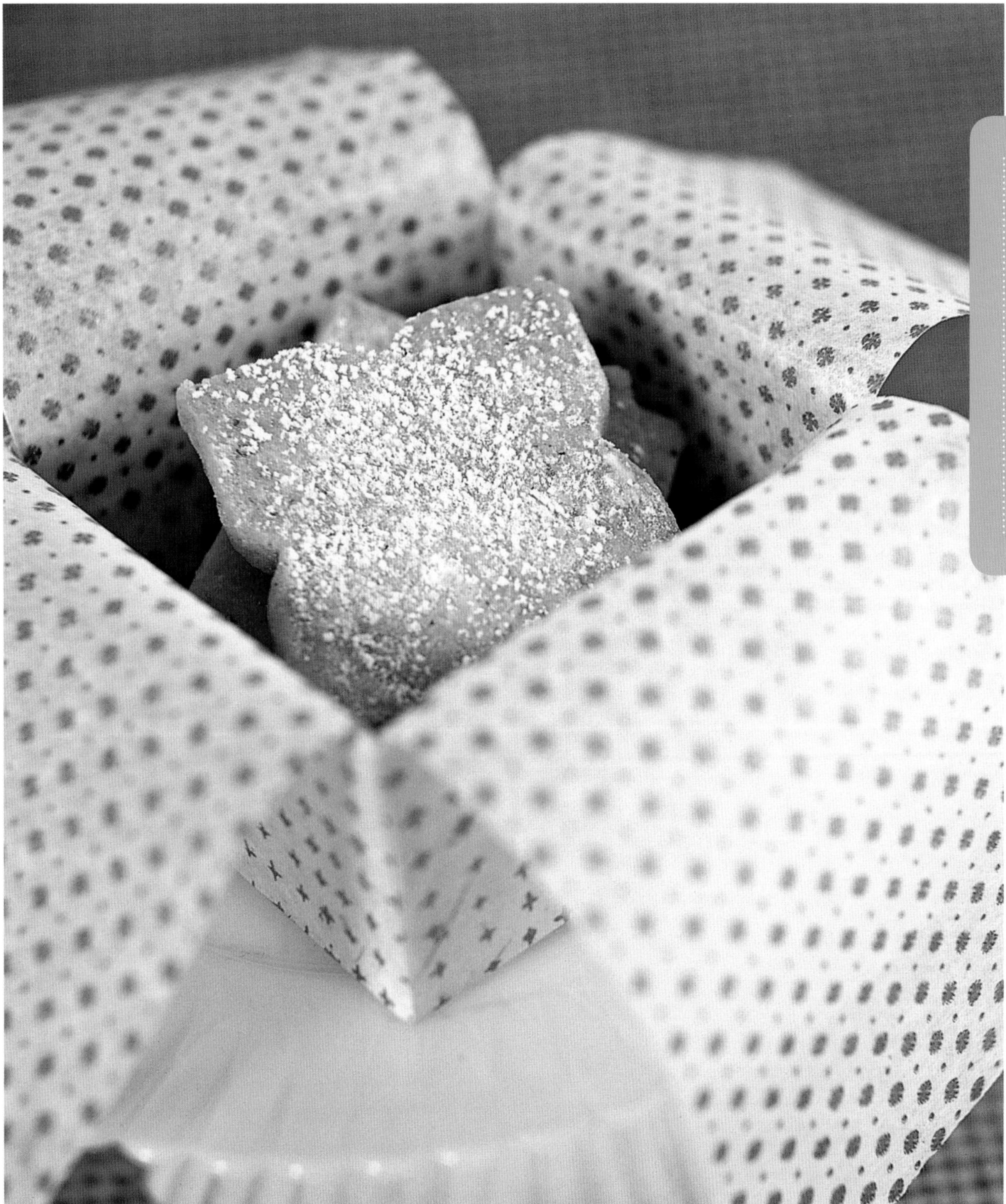

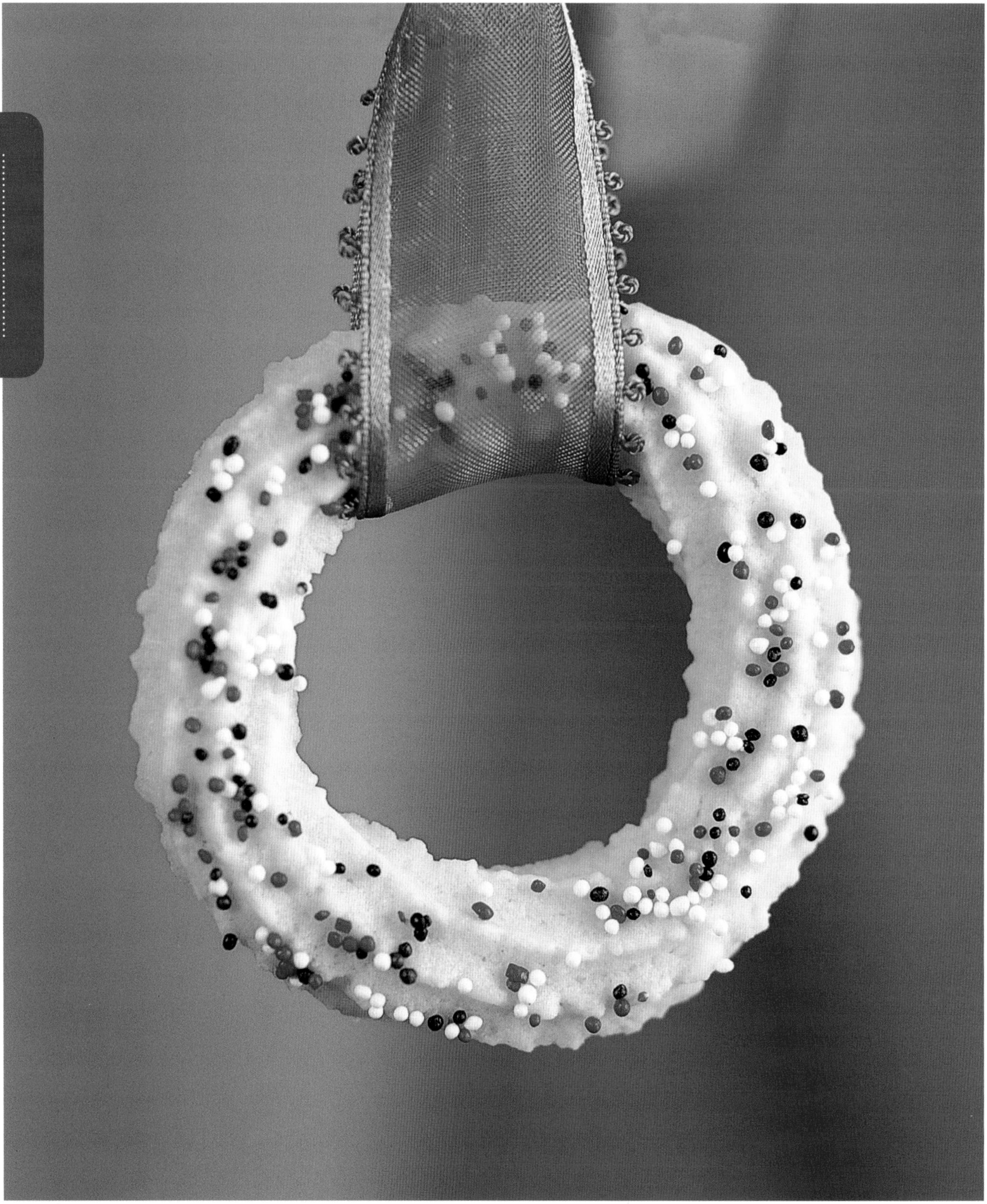

SPRITZ COOKIES

MAKES
6
DOZEN

To speed up the task of making these buttery Swedish cookies, use the 1-inch-wide ridged cutter on the press to squirt out the dough in long strips directly onto the baking sheet, bake them until crisp, and then cut them on the diagonal while still hot from the oven.

Ingredients:

1 cup unsalted butter,
(at room temperature)
3⁄4 cup sugar
1 egg
1 teaspoon vanilla extract
1 teaspoon almond extract
2 cups plus 2 tablespoons
all-purpose flour
Dash of salt

Directions:

1. Preheat the oven to 350°F.
2. Lightly grease baking sheets.
3. In a bowl, using an electric mixer or a spoon, beat the butter until creamy.
4. Gradually add the sugar and beat until light. Mix in the egg and the vanilla and almond extracts.
5. Add the flour and salt, mixing until smooth.
6. Pack the dough into a cookie press fitted with a star or ridged tip or any desired design.
7. Press out the dough onto the prepared baking sheets.
8. One sheet at a time, bake the cookies for 8 to 10 minutes, or until the edges are golden brown.
9. If the 1-inch-wide ridged cutter is used, immediately cut the strips crosswise on the diagonal to make 11⁄2-inch-long cookies.
10. Transfer to racks to cool.

PEPPARKAKOR

MAKES
3
DOZEN

Cutters in the shapes of pigs and goats are typically used in Finland and Sweden for cutting out these very thin, very crisp, pleasantly spicy Scandinavian holiday cookies. Some bakers like to dip the heads and hooves in melted white chocolate for a tasty accent. Little piglets are fun for children to cut out and dip to make chocolate snouts.

Ingredients:

1⁄2 cup unsalted butter,
(at room temperature)
3⁄4 cup sugar
1 1⁄2 tablespoons light corn syrup
1 egg
1⁄2 teaspoon baking soda
1⁄4 teaspoon salt
1 teaspoon ground cinnamon
1 teaspoon ground ginger
1⁄2 teaspoon ground allspice
1⁄2 teaspoon ground cloves
1 1⁄2 cups all-purpose flour

Directions:

PART 1:

1. In a large bowl, using an electric mixer or a spoon, cream together the butter, sugar, corn syrup, egg, baking soda, salt, cinnamon, ginger, allspice, and cloves until smooth.
2. Stir in the flour.
3. Scrape out the dough onto a sheet of plastic wrap and flatten into a disk, using the wrap, not your fingers.
4. Wrap and chill for about 30 minutes, or until firm.

PART 2:

1. Preheat the oven to 350°F.
2. Lightly grease baking sheets, or use nonstick or parchment-lined baking sheets.
3. On a lightly floured surface, roll out the dough 1⁄8 inch thick.
4. Using 2 1⁄2-inch cutters in desired shapes, cut out the cookies and transfer them to the prepared baking sheets, spacing them about 1 inch apart.
5. One sheet at a time, bake the cookies for 10 minutes, or until light brown.
6. Transfer to racks to cool.

FRENCH LEMON WAFERS

A lovely citrus scent rises from a plate
of these pretty wafers.

MAKES
3
DOZEN

Ingredients:

1 cup chilled unsalted butter

1 1/4 cups powdered sugar

2 egg yolks

2 teaspoons grated lemon zest
or orange zest

1 tablespoon lemon juice
or orange liqueur

2 cups all-purpose flour

1 teaspoon baking soda

1 teaspoon cream of tartar

Directions:

1. In a food processor or in a bowl, combine the butter and sugar
   and pulse or mix with an electric mixer until crumbly.
2. Add the egg yolks, citrus zest, and lemon juice or liqueur and
   process or mix until the mixture comes together.
3. In a bowl, stir together the flour, baking soda, and cream of tartar.
4. Add the flour mixture to the butter mixture and process or mix
   until blended.
5. Scrape out half of the dough onto a sheet of plastic wrap and,
   using the wrap, not your fingers, shape into a log about 2 inches
   in diameter.
6. Repeat with a second sheet of plastic wrap and the remaining dough.
7. Wrap and chill for about 1 hour, or until firm.
8. Preheat the oven to 350°F.
9. Line baking sheets with parchment paper, or use nonstick
   baking sheets.
10. Slice the logs into rounds 3/16 inch thick.
11. Place on the prepared baking sheets, spacing them about
    1 1/2 inches apart.
12. One sheet at a time, bake the cookies for 8 to 10 minutes,
    or until golden brown.
13. Transfer to racks to cool.

FROSTY SNOWMEN

MAKES
6
DOZEN

A shiny transparent glaze perfumed with lemon juice and raspberry liqueur sheaths these tender butter cookies. It is fun to cut out other decorative holiday shapes, such as stars, bells, bears, angels, or trees.

Ingredients:

1 cup powdered sugar
1 cup unsalted butter,
(at room temperature)
1 egg yolk
2 teaspoons grated lemon zest
2 1/4 cups all-purpose flour
1/8 teaspoon salt

GLAZE:
2 cups powdered sugar
2 tablespoons fresh lemon juice
1 tablespoon Framboise or water

Directions:

1. In a bowl, cream together the sugar, butter, egg yolk, and lemon zest until light.
2. Add the flour and salt and mix quickly to form a dough.
3. Gather into a ball, wrap in plastic wrap, and chill for 20 minutes, or until firm.
4. Preheat the oven to 375°F.
5. Line baking sheets with parchment paper, or use nonstick baking sheets.
6. On a lightly floured surface, roll out the dough about 3/16 inch thick.
7. Using a 2 1/2-inch snowman cutter, cut out cookies.
8. Place on the prepared baking sheets, spacing them 2 inches apart.
9. One sheet at a time, bake the cookies for 8 to 10 minutes, or until golden brown.
10. Transfer to racks to cool.
11. Make the glaze (see below).
12. Using an icing spatula, spread the icing on the cooled cookies.
13. Let the cookies stand until the icing is set.

FOR THE GLAZE:
In a bowl, stir together the sugar and lemon juice and Framboise or water to make a thin, transparent glaze. If necessary, add a few drops of hot water to achieve the desired consistency.

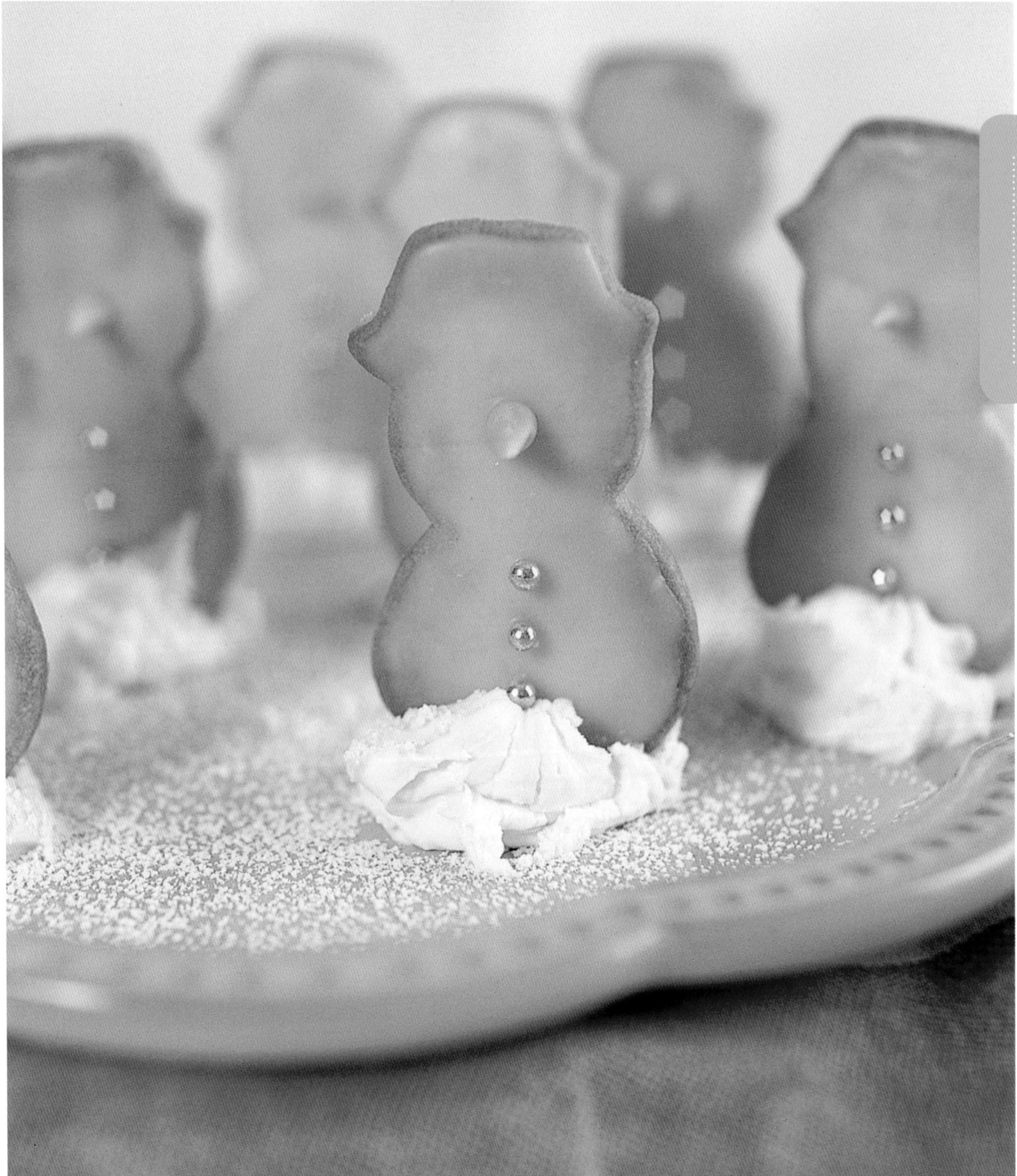

FROSTED CRANBERRY-ORANGE COOKIES

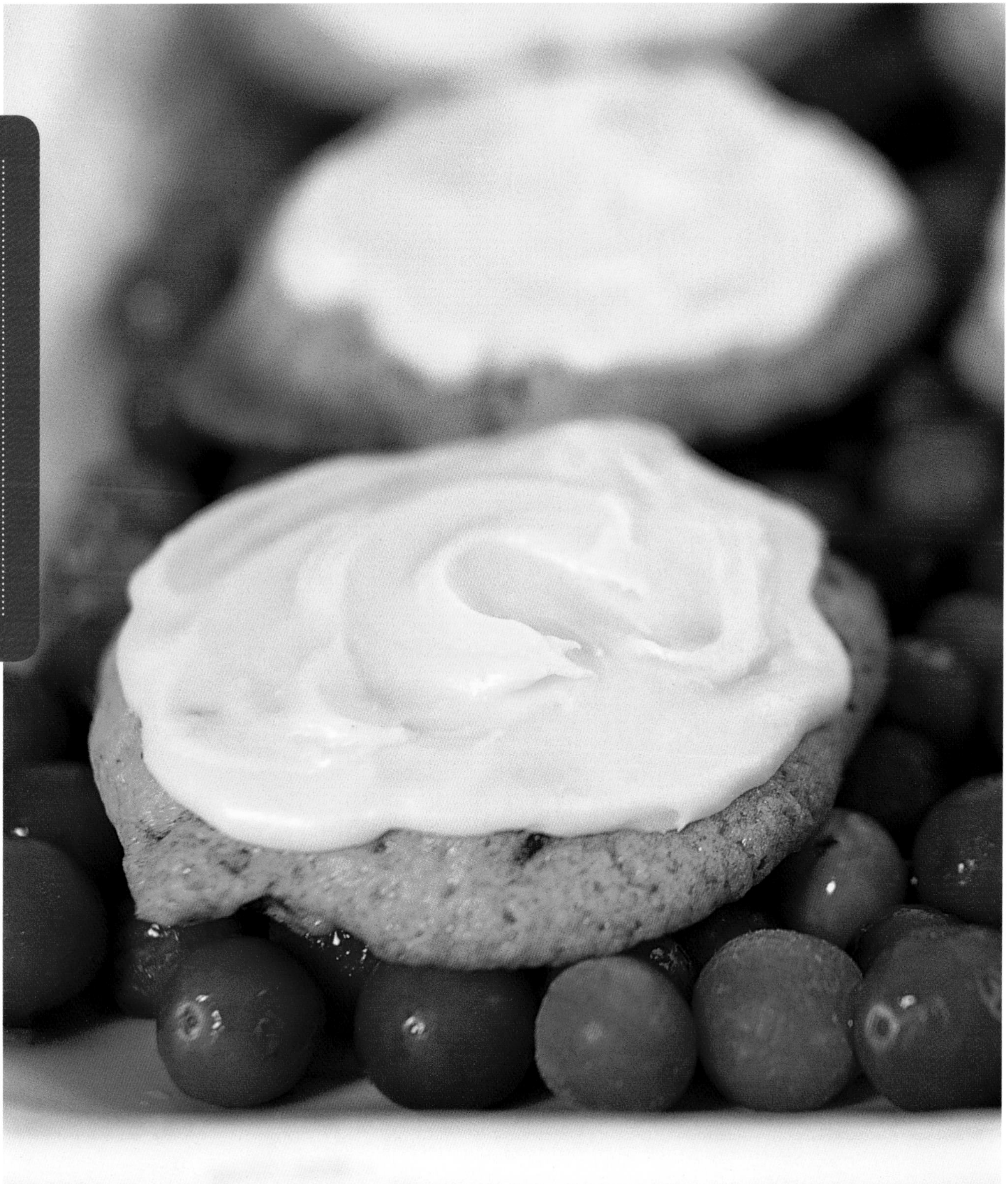

FROSTED CRANBERRY-ORANGE COOKIES

MAKES
3
DOZEN

Tart-sweet cranberries lace these soft and chewy, orange-flavored cookies.

Ingredients:

6 tablespoons unsalted butter,
(at room temperature)
1/2 cup granulated sugar
1/4 cup firmly packed light
brown sugar
1 egg
2 teaspoons grated orange zest
3 tablespoons thawed frozen orange
juice concentrate
1 1/3 cups all-purpose flour
1/2 teaspoon baking powder
1/4 teaspoon baking soda
1/2 teaspoon ground cloves
1/4 teaspoon salt
1 cup dried cranberries
1/2 cup coarsely chopped raw
pistachios or walnuts

ORANGE ICING:

1 1/2 cups powdered sugar
3 tablespoons unsalted butter, melted
2 tablespoons thawed frozen orange
juice concentrate

Directions:

1. Preheat the oven to 375°F.
2. Lightly grease baking sheets.
3. In a large bowl, using an electric mixer or a spoon,
   cream together the butter and sugars until light.
4. Add the egg, orange zest, and orange juice concentrate
   and beat until blended.
5. In another bowl, stir together the flour, baking powder,
   baking soda, cloves, and salt.
6. Add the flour mixture to the butter mixture and mix
   until blended.
7. Stir in the cranberries and nuts.
8. Drop the dough by rounded spoonfuls onto the prepared
   baking sheets.
9. Bake the cookies for 10 to 12 minutes, or until golden brown.
10. Cool on racks.

FOR THE ICING:

1. In a bowl, stir together the powdered sugar, butter,
   and orange juice concentrate until smooth.
2. Spread on the cooled cookies.

CHOCOLATE-PECAN CARAMEL CANDY BARS

MAKES
40
COOKIES

A swirled chocolate-caramel topping crowns these heavenly bars.

Ingredients:

CRUST:

1 1/2 cups all-purpose flour
1/2 cup firmly packed light
brown sugar
1/2 cup chilled unsalted butter

TOPPING:

6 tablespoons unsalted butter,
(at room temperature)
1 cup firmly packed dark
brown sugar
3 tablespoons honey
3 tablespoons heavy cream
2 tablespoons maple syrup
1 1/2 cups chopped pecans
or walnuts
1/2 cup (3 ounces) semisweet
chocolate chips

Directions:

1. Preheat the oven to 350°F.
2. Line a 9-by-13-inch baking pan with aluminum foil and grease the foil.
3. To make the crust, combine the flour and sugar and pulse briefly or stir to mix, in a food processor or in a bowl.
4. Add the butter and process or mix until crumbly.
5. Transfer to the prepared pan and pat evenly onto the bottom of the pan.
6. Bake for 12 minutes.
7. Transfer the pan to a rack.
8. Leave the oven set at 350°F.
9. Make the topping and pour on top. (See below.)
10. Return the pan to the oven and bake for 12 to 15 minutes, or until the caramel layer is bubbly.
11. Remove from the oven and sprinkle with the chocolate chips.
12. Let melt for 1 to 2 minutes, then swirl with a spatula.
13. Let cool.
14. Invert the baked sheet onto a rack, lift off the pan, and peel off the foil.
15. Cut into 1 1/2-by-2-inch bars.

FOR THE TOPPING:

1. In a saucepan, heat the butter over low heat until it melts and bubbles.
2. Add the brown sugar, honey, cream, and maple syrup and bring to a boil over medium heat, stirring constantly.
3. Let boil without stirring for 1 minute.
4. Pour over the hot crust and sprinkle evenly with the nuts.

BUTTERSCOTCH-PISTACHIO BARS

MAKES
5
DOZEN

Vary these blondie bars with your favorite nut-and-candy combination. Pecans and chocolate chips or pistachios and butterscotch chips make winning duos.

Ingredients:

1 cup plus 2 tablespoons
unsalted butter,
(at room temperature)
2 3/4 cups firmly packed light
brown sugar
1 1/2 teaspoons vanilla extract
3 eggs
3 cups all-purpose flour
1 1/2 teaspoons baking powder
3/4 teaspoon baking soda
1/2 teaspoon salt
3/4 cup whole raw pistachio nuts
or chopped pecans
1 1/3 cups (8 ounces) butterscotch
chips, or 8 ounces bittersweet
chocolate or milk chocolate,
chopped

Directions:

1. Preheat the oven to 350°F.
2. Lightly grease a 10-by-15-inch baking pan.
3. In a large bowl, using an electric mixer or a spoon, cream together the butter and sugar until light.
4. Mix in the vanilla and eggs until blended.
5. In another bowl, stir together the flour, baking powder, baking soda, and salt.
6. Add the flour mixture to the butter mixture until well mixed.
7. Stir in the nuts and butterscotch chips or chocolate.
8. Spread evenly in the prepared pan.
9. Bake for 20 to 25 minutes, or until set and golden brown.
10. Transfer the pan to a rack to cool.
11. Cut into 1 1/2-inch squares.

SNAP-CRACKLE GINGERSNAPS

MAKES
4
DOZEN

German housewives have long been making this holiday recipe. The crackly cookies can be packed in a reusable widemouthed jar with a clamp-down lid and tied with a bright ribbon. They are good keepers.

Ingredients:

3⁄4 cup unsalted butter,
(at room temperature)
1⁄2 cup granulated sugar
1⁄2 cup firmly packed light
brown sugar
1 egg
1⁄4 cup dark molasses
2 cups all-purpose flour
1 1⁄2 teaspoons baking soda
1⁄2 teaspoon salt
2 teaspoons ground ginger
1 teaspoon ground cinnamon
Raw sugar for coating

Directions:

1. In a large bowl, using an electric mixer or a spoon, cream together the butter and sugars until light.
2. Add the egg and molasses and mix until smooth.
3. In another bowl, stir together the flour, baking soda, salt, ginger, and cinnamon.
4. Add the flour mixture to the butter mixture and mix until smooth.
5. Cover and chill for 30 minutes, or until firm.
6. Preheat the oven to 325°F.
7. Lightly grease baking sheets, or use nonstick baking sheets.
8. Pour some raw sugar into a small bowl.
9. Roll the dough into 1-inch balls between your palms, and roll in the raw sugar to coat lightly.
10. Place on the prepared baking sheets, spacing them about 2 inches apart.
11. One sheet at a time, bake the cookies for 10 minutes, or just until brown on the edges and still barely soft in the center.
12. Transfer to racks to cool completely, or serve slightly warm.

MACADAMIA-GINGER BISCOTTI BATONS

MAKES
4
DOZEN

These crispy, wafer-thin, nine-inch-long cookies are the aussie's nod to biscotti. They look particularly dramatic wrapped in clear cellophane and gaily tied with ribbon, and they are an excellent shipper.

Ingredients:

4 egg whites

Dash of salt

2/3 cup sugar

1/2 teaspoon ground ginger

1 tablespoon grated fresh ginger

1/4 teaspoon almond extract

1 teaspoon vanilla extract

1 1/4 cups all-purpose flour

1 1/4 cups (7 ounces) macadamia nuts, almonds, or toasted, skinned hazelnuts

(page 15)

Directions:

1. Preheat the oven to 300°F.
2. Butter and flour a 9-inch square pan.
3. In a large bowl, using an electric stand mixer fitted with a whip attachment or using a whisk, beat the egg whites and salt until frothy.
4. Gradually add the sugar and beat until stiff peaks form.
5. Mix in the ground and fresh ginger and the almond and vanilla extracts.
6. Fold in the flour and nuts.
7. Spread evenly in the prepared pan.
8. Bake for 30 minutes, or until set and very faintly brown on the bottom.
9. Remove from the oven, invert onto a rack, lift off the pan, and let cool for 15 minutes.
10. Reduce the oven temperature to 150°F.
11. Slice the baked sheet as thinly as possible, about 3/16 inch thick, making long, slender slices.
12. Lay the slices flat on 2 ungreased baking sheets and return to the oven.
13. Bake for 30 minutes, or until light brown.
14. Turn off the oven and let the cookies dry in the oven for 1 hour longer.

APRICOT-WALNUT SQUARES

MAKES
4
DOZEN

These chewy apricot bars are a popular teatime and holiday party treat.

Ingredients:

1 1/2 cups dried apricots
1 1/2 cups water

CRUST:
1/3 cup firmly packed dark
brown sugar
1 1/2 cups all-purpose flour
3/4 cup chilled unsalted butter,
cut into pieces

TOPPING:
3 eggs
1 1/2 cups firmly packed light
brown sugar
1 tablespoon Amaretto or rum
1/2 cup all-purpose flour
1 teaspoon baking powder
1/4 teaspoon ground cloves
1/4 teaspoon salt
3/4 cup chopped walnuts or pecans
Powdered sugar for dusting

Directions:

PART 1:
1. Preheat the oven to 350°F.
2. Grease a 9-by-12-inch baking pan.
3. Place the apricots and water in a small saucepan.
4. Bring to a simmer and cover. Simmer for 10 minutes, or until softened.
5. Drain, let cool, chop, and set aside.
6. Make the crust (see below).
7. While crust is baking, make the topping (see below).
8. Remove the crust from the oven and spread the topping evenly over the surface.
9. Return to the oven and continue baking for 25 to 30 minutes, or until set.
10. Transfer the pan to a rack to cool.
11. Dust with powdered sugar.
12. Cut into 1 1/2-inch squares.

FOR CRUST:
1. To make the crust, combine the sugar and flour and pulse briefly or stir to mix, in a food processor or in a bowl.
2. Add the butter and process or mix with an electric mixer until crumbly.
3. Pat into the prepared pan. Bake for 15 minutes.

FOR THE TOPPING:
1. In an electric mixer, beat the eggs until light in color.
2. Beat in the brown sugar and liqueur or rum.
3. In another bowl, stir together the flour, baking powder, cloves, and salt.
4. Add the flour mixture to the egg mixture and mix well.
5. Stir in the nuts and apricots.

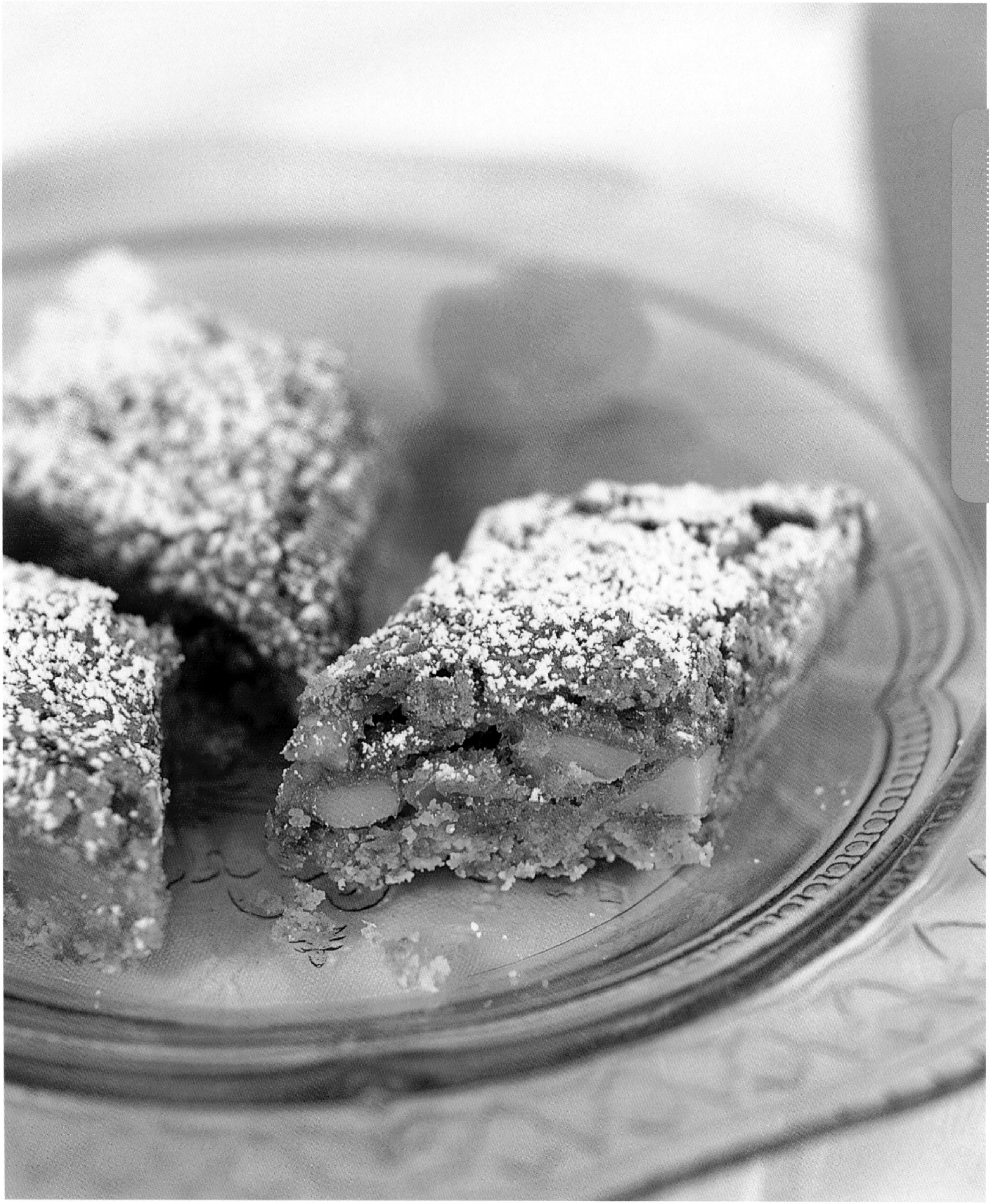

CANDIED ORANGE PEEL

MAKES
2
CUPS

A thick and zesty lemon layer glazes a shortbread crust for these melt-in-the-mouth sweets, a lovely and tasty addition to any Christmas cookie platter.

Ingredients:

4 oranges
1 1/3 cups sugar
1 1/4 cups water

Directions:

1. Peel the oranges, removing the peel in quarters.
2. Use the fruit for another purpose.
3. Place the peels in a saucepan, add water to cover, and bring to a boil.
4. Drain and discard the water.
5. Again add water to cover, and return to a boil.
6. Drain the water again and repeat one more time.
7. Drain and let the orange peel cool slightly.
8. With a spoon, scrape off most of the white pith from the peels.
9. In a medium saucepan, bring the sugar and the 1 1/4 cups water to a boil, stirring until sugar is dissolved.
10. Add the peels and simmer, uncovered, for about 20 minutes, or until the liquid is fully absorbed.
11. Transfer the candied orange peel to a rack and let stand until dry.

VANILLA PECAN FINGERS

MAKES
5
DOZEN

Stack these snowy white bars on a holiday cookie platter. Your guests won't be able to resist them.

Ingredients:

2 cups pecans

1⁄3 cup powdered sugar

1 vanilla bean, split lengthwise

1 cup unsalted butter,
(at room temperature)

1 teaspoon vanilla extract

1 tablespoon water

1 3⁄4 cups all-purpose flour

1⁄4 teaspoon salt

Powdered sugar for dusting

Directions:

1. Preheat the oven to 250°F.
2. Lightly grease baking sheets, or use nonstick baking sheets.
3. In a blender or food processor, finely grind the nuts with 1 tablespoon of the sugar.
4. Place the remaining sugar in a medium-sized bowl and, using the tip of a sharp knife, scrape the seeds from the vanilla bean into the sugar.
5. Add the butter and, using an electric mixer, cream together until light and fluffy.
6. Stir in the vanilla and water.
7. In another bowl, stir together the flour, ground nuts, and salt.
8. Add the flour mixture to the butter mixture and mix until blended.
9. Spoon out rounded teaspoonfuls of the dough and shape into logs about 3⁄4 inch wide and 1 3⁄4 inches long.
10. Place on the prepared baking sheets, spacing them about 1 1⁄2 inches apart.
11. Bake for 50 to 60 minutes, or until a very light brown.
12. Transfer to a rack to cool for a few minutes.
13. Dust a sheet of waxed paper with a thin layer of powdered sugar shaken through a sieve, and transfer the warm cookies to it.
14. Sift more sugar over the tops to coat completely.

GIANDUIA SNOWBALLS

MAKES
2
DOZEN

These big, plump chocolate bonbons, with their soft centers and crackled shiny exteriors, melt in the mouth. For a holiday party, show off these gems by stacking them high on a pedestal plate. Do not overbake them: their soft centers are the secret to their goodness.

Ingredients:

2 eggs

6 tablespoons sugar

9 ounces bittersweet chocolate, or 1 1/2 cups semisweet chocolate chips

2 tablespoons unsalted butter

1 teaspoon vanilla extract

1/2 cup all-purpose flour

1/8 teaspoon salt

1/2 teaspoon baking powder

1 1/4 cups (7 1/2 ounces) semisweet chocolate chips

1 cup coarsely chopped toasted, skinned hazelnuts (page 15), walnuts, pecans, or chopped toffee

Directions:

1. In an electric stand mixer fitted with a whip attachment, beat the eggs and sugar until thick and light, about 6 minutes.
2. In the top pan of a double boiler, combine the chocolate or chocolate chips and butter.
3. Place over hot water in the lower pan and heat until melted.
4. Stir until blended.
5. Remove from over the water and let cool completely.
6. Stir the cooled chocolate into the egg mixture.
7. Add the vanilla and mix well.
8. In another bowl, stir together the flour, salt, and baking powder.
9. Add the flour mixture to the egg mixture and mix well.
10. Stir in the chocolate chips and nuts.
11. Line a baking sheet with parchment paper, or use a nonstick baking sheet.
12. Using a 1 3/4-inch scoop, scoop the dough into rounded balls and drop onto the prepared baking sheet, spacing them about 1 1/2 inches apart.
13. Do not flatten the balls.
14. Place the baking sheet in the freezer for 30 minutes to firm them up.
15. Preheat the oven to 350°F.
16. Bake for 10 to 12 minutes, or until set but still soft inside. Do not overbake.
17. Transfer to racks to cool.

ALMOND TILES

MAKES
2
DOZEN

This paper-thin, crispy wafer is shaped around a rolling pin to form its typical clay-roof-tile shape. It is one of the most popular of all French cookies, and is often featured on the cookie plates in France's finer restaurants.

Ingredients:

3 tablespoons unsalted butter
1/2 cup sugar
2 egg whites
1/4 teaspoon vanilla extract
1/4 teaspoon almond extract
1/4 cup all-purpose flour
1 cup sliced almonds

Directions:

1. Preheat the oven to 400°F.
2. Heavily grease baking sheets.
3. In a small saucepan, heat the butter over low heat until it begins to melt.
4. Remove from the heat to finish melting.
5. Let cool.
6. In a small bowl, combine the sugar, egg whites, and vanilla and almond extracts.
7. Whisk lightly just to mix.
8. Stir in the flour until smooth.
9. Add the melted butter, whisking until smooth.
10. Stir in 3/4 cup of the almonds.
11. Drop the batter onto the prepared baking sheets by teaspoonfuls and spread with the back of the spoon into rounds 3 inches in diameter.
12. The cookies should be spaced 2 inches apart.
13. Sprinkle with the remaining sliced almonds.
14. One sheet at a time, bake the cookies for 5 to 7 minutes, or until golden brown on the edges.
15. Quickly remove the cookies from the baking sheet using a long metal spatula, and drape them over a rolling pin.
16. Let cool.

TIP:
If the cookies should harden before you remove them from the baking sheet, return the sheet to the oven for 30 seconds to soften them. When the cookies are cool, after 30 to 60 seconds, remove them from the rolling pin.

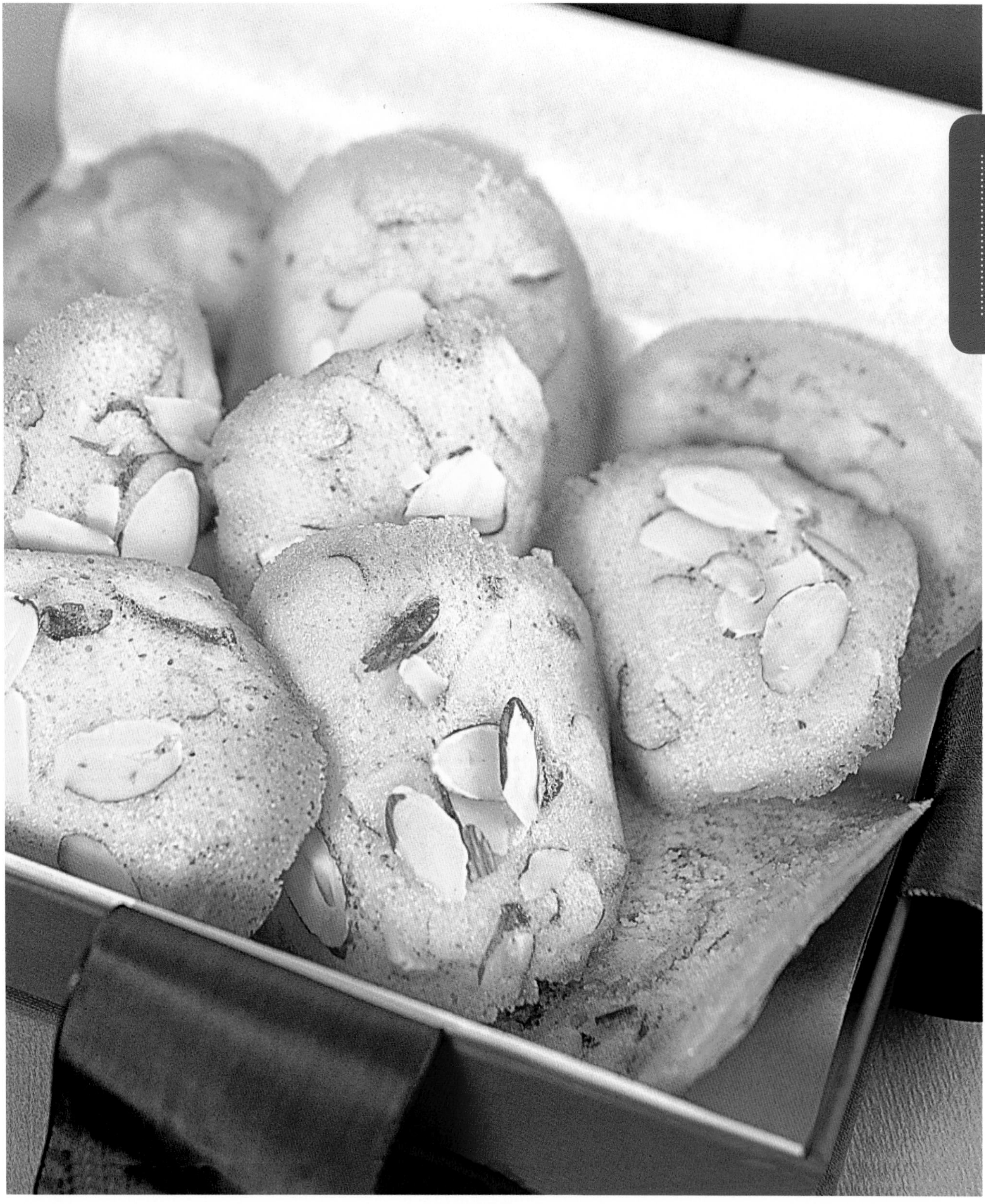

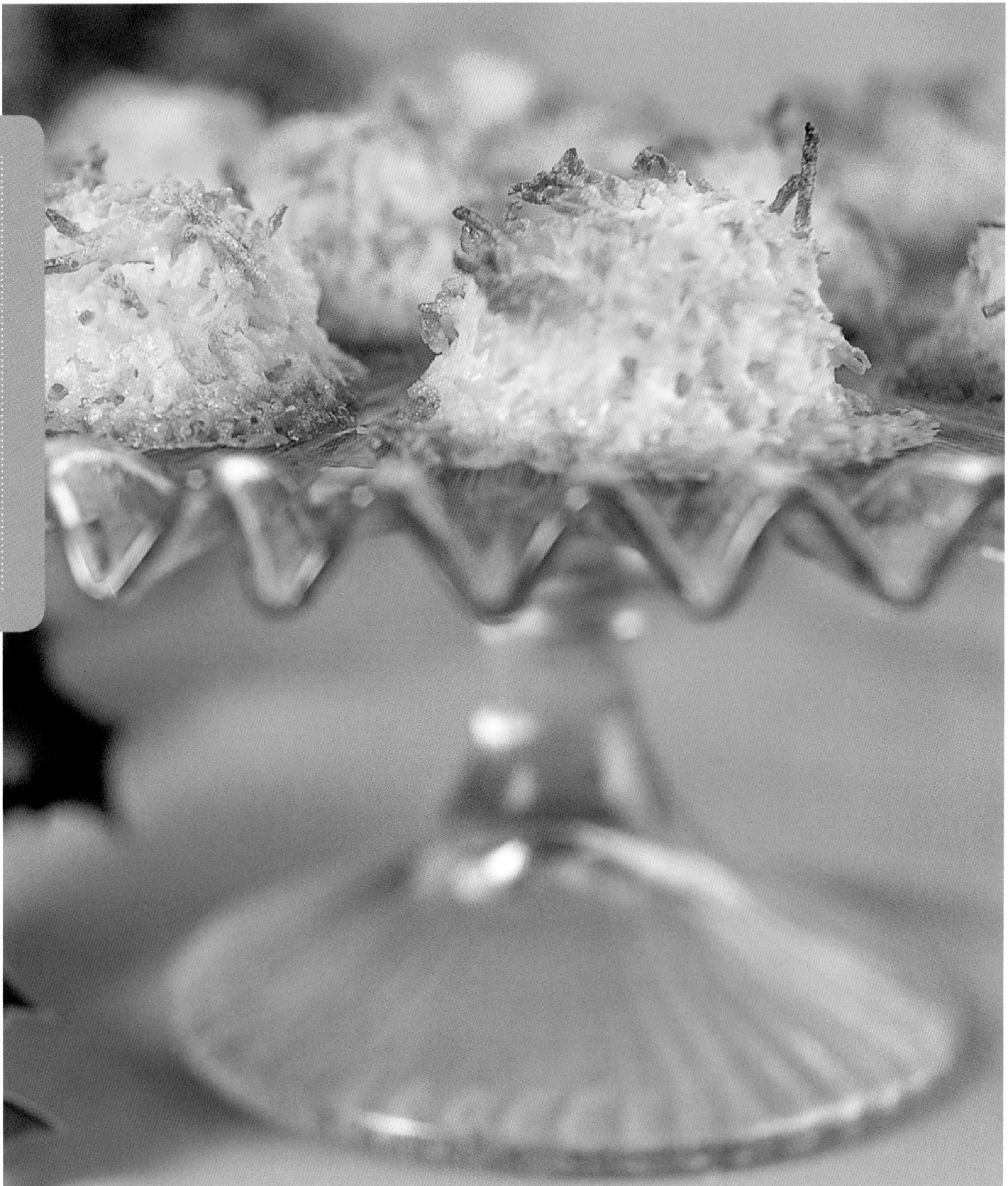

CHEWY COCONUT ORANGE MACAROONS

MAKES
3
DOZEN

A whole egg lends a pale golden color and rich flavor to these billowy coconut rounds. With their snowball shape, they fit the holiday motif.

Ingredients:

1 egg
2⁄3 cup sugar
1 teaspoon vanilla extract
1 tablespoon grated orange zest
2 1⁄2 cups sweetened shredded coconut

Directions:

1. Preheat the oven to 350°F.
2. Line baking sheets with parchment paper, or use nonstick baking sheets.
3. In a bowl, using an electric mixer, preferably fitted with a whip attachment, beat the egg until light.
4. Gradually beat in the sugar, vanilla, and orange zest.
5. Continue beating until light and fluffy.
6. Fold in the coconut.
7. Drop the batter by heaping teaspoonfuls onto the prepared baking sheets, making mounds and spacing them about 1 1⁄2 inches apart.
8. Bake for 15 minutes.
9. Turn off the heat and let the cookies dry in the oven for 10 minutes longer.
10. The insides of the cookies should still be soft, while the outer surface is crispy.
11. Transfer to racks to cool.

MACADAMIA-WHITE CHOCOLATE BROWNIES

MAKES 5 DOZEN

For a gala Christmas party, this expanded brownie recipe is ideal for turning out a big batch of rich bites swiftly. Sugar-sweet macadamia nuts and white chocolate chips enhance each mouthful. These are a crowd-pleaser for adults and children alike.

Ingredients:

6 ounces bittersweet or
semisweet chocolate
1 cup unsalted butter
1 1/4 cups all-purpose flour
2/3 cup unsweetened cocoa powder
1 1/2 teaspoons baking powder
1/4 teaspoon salt
6 eggs
2 1/4 cups sugar
2 teaspoons vanilla extract
1 cup (6 ounces) white
chocolate chips
1 1/4 cups macadamia nuts,
chopped

Directions:

1. Preheat the oven to 350°F.
2. Line a 10-by-15-inch pan with aluminum foil, shiny side up, and grease lightly.
3. In the top pan of a double boiler, combine the chocolate and butter.
4. Place over the lower pan of hot water and heat until melted, then stir until smooth and let cool.
5. In a bowl, stir together the flour, cocoa, baking powder, and salt.
6. In the large bowl of an electric stand mixer fitted with a whip attachment, beat the eggs until light and fluffy.
7. Beat in the sugar and vanilla, mixing well.
8. Stir in the melted chocolate and the flour mixture.
9. Stir in the white chocolate chips and 3/4 cup of the nuts.
10. Spread in the prepared pan and sprinkle with the remaining nuts.
11. Bake for 25 to 30 minutes, or just until barely set.
12. Let cool in the pan on a rack, then cut into 1 1/2-inch squares.

VARIATION:
For an everyday brownie, omit the macadamia nuts and white chocolate chips and add 1 1/4 cups chopped walnuts or pecans and 1 cup (6 ounces) double or semisweet chocolate chips.

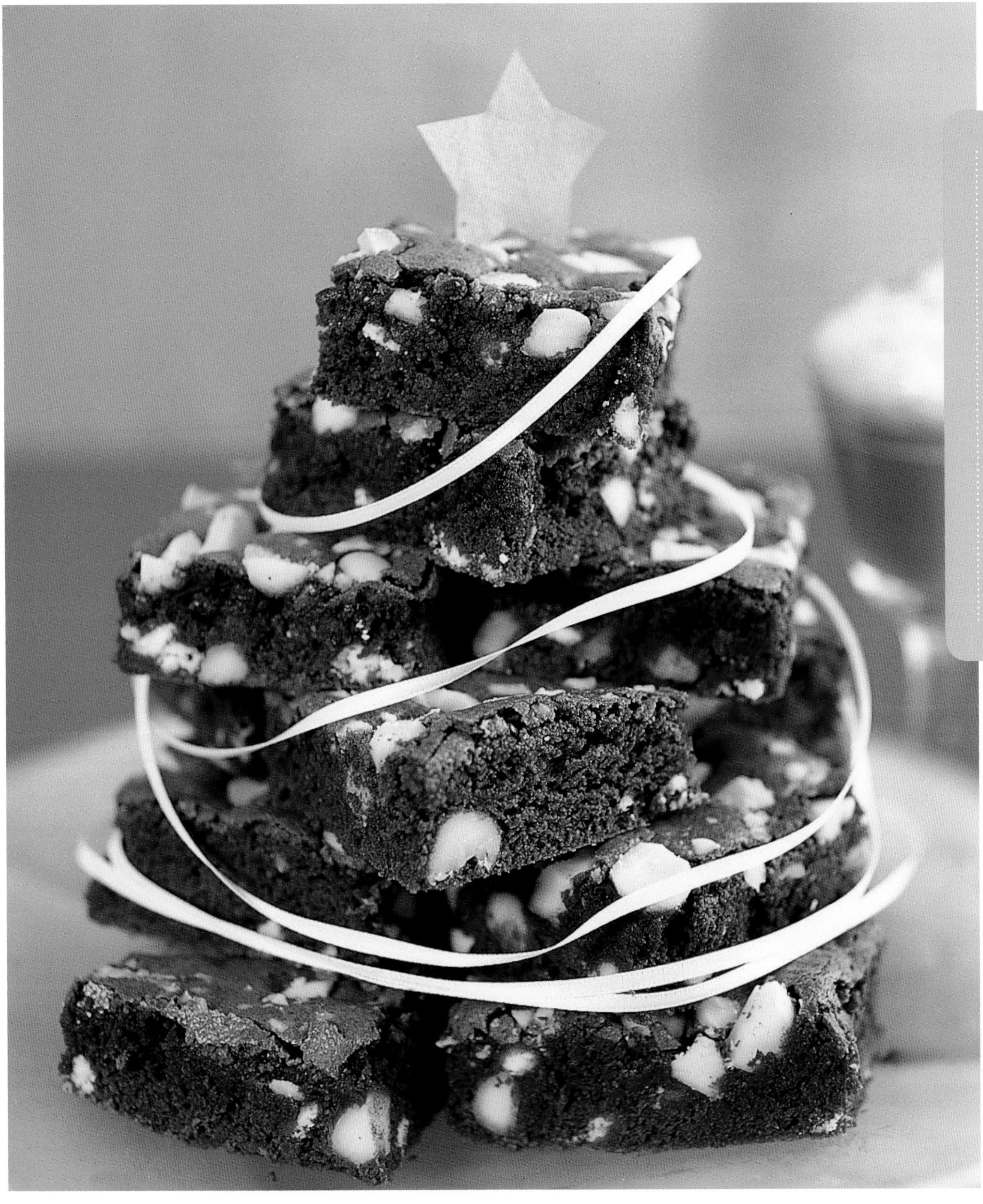

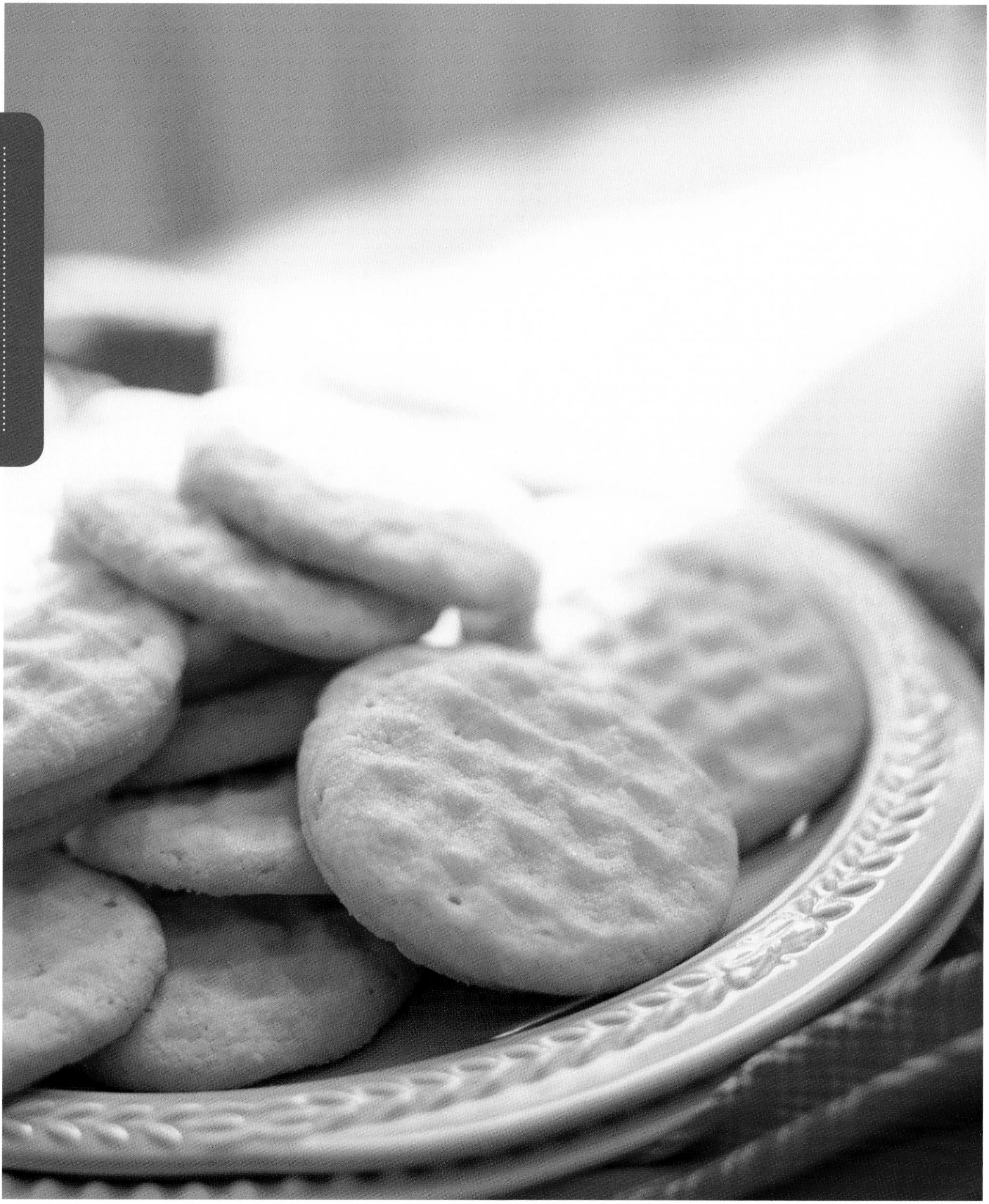

PEANUT BUTTER COOKIES

MAKES
3
DOZEN

Peanut butter cookies are as American as apple pie, and are a must-have for any holiday table. To give your cookies that "traditional" look, use a fork to make the crisscross design on top.

Ingredients:

1/2 cup butter
1/2 cup crunchy peanut butter
1/2 cup sugar
1/2 cup packed light brown sugar
1 egg
1 1/4 cups all-purpose flour
3/4 tsp baking soda
1/2 tsp baking powder
1/4 tsp salt

Directions:

PART 1

1. Blend together the butter, peanut butter, and the white and brown sugars.
2. Beat in the egg.
3. In a separate bowl, combine the flour, baking soda, baking powder, and salt.
4. Gradually add to butter mixture.
5. Cover and refrigerate dough for at least one hour.

PART 2

1. Preheat oven to 375°F.
2. Roll dough into 1-inch balls.
3. Place on greased cookie sheet.
4. Flatten with a fork dipped in flour to form crisscross pattern.
5. Bake for 10-12 minutes, until lightly golden.
6. Remove from baking sheets and cool on wire rack.

TANGY LEMON SQUARES

MAKES
4
DOZEN

A thick and zesty lemon layer glazes a shortbread crust for these melt-in-the-mouth sweets, a lovely and tasty addition to any Christmas cookie platter.

Ingredients:

SHORTBREAD CRUST:

2 cups all-purpose flour

1/2 cup powdered sugar

1 cup chilled unsalted butter

LEMON TOPPING:

5 eggs

2 cups granulated sugar

6 tablespoons all-purpose flour

4 teaspoons grated lemon zest

3/4 cup fresh lemon juice

Powdered sugar for dusting

Directions:

1. Preheat the oven to 350°F.
2. Have ready an ungreased 9-by-12-inch baking pan.
3. To make the crust, combine the flour and sugar and pulse briefly or stir to mix, in a food processor or in a bowl.
4. Add the butter and process or mix with an electric mixer until crumbly.
5. Pat into the baking pan.
6. Bake for 12 to 14 minutes, or until a light golden brown.
7. Let cool on a rack for 3 to 4 minutes.
8. Reduce the oven temperature to 325°F.
9. Return the pan to the oven and continue baking for 25 to 30 minutes, or until just set.
10. Transfer to a rack to cool for a few minutes.
11. While still warm, dust with powdered sugar shaken through a sieve.
12. Let cool completely, then cut into 1 1/2-inch squares.
13. These are best if served within a day or two.
14. Store in an airtight container in the refrigerator.

FOR THE TOPPING:

1. In a large bowl, using an electric mixer or a whisk, beat the eggs until light in color.
2. In a bowl, stir together the sugar and flour.
3. Add the flour mixture to the eggs and mix until blended.
4. Stir in the lemon zest and juice, mixing until smooth.
5. Pour over the slightly cooled crust.

NORWEGIAN LACE COOKIES

MAKES
4
DOZEN

These see-through cookies have a wonderful chewy caramel crunch—perfect to accompany a platter of fresh fruit or homemade honey ice cream. Bake them on a dry day; otherwise they may absorb moisture and lose their brittle caramel bite. The secret is to bake them on aluminum foil; they peel off easily once cool.

Ingredients:

1/2 cup firmly packed light brown sugar
6 tablespoons unsalted butter
3 tablespoons honey
1 tablespoon heavy cream
1/4 teaspoon salt
1/4 teaspoon ground cloves
1/4 teaspoon ground ginger
1/2 cup all-purpose flour
3/4 cup regular rolled oats

Directions:

1. Preheat the oven to 375°F.
2. Line baking sheets with aluminum foil, then generously grease the foil.
3. In a saucepan, combine the sugar, butter, honey, cream, salt, cloves, and ginger.
4. Heat over medium heat until bubbly.
5. Remove from the heat and stir in the flour and oats.
6. Drop the dough by teaspoonfuls onto the prepared sheets, spacing them about 4 inches apart.
7. One sheet at a time, bake the cookies for 6 minutes, or until golden brown.
8. Transfer the baking sheets to racks to cool for 1 minute.
9. Then slip the foil along with the cookies onto a countertop and let cool completely.
10. Peel off the cookies from the foil.

SNOWBALL COOKIES

MAKES
32
COOKIES

The coconut coating gives this old-fashioned ball cookie a little modern-day flair.

Ingredients:

12 ounces white chocolate chips

1/4 cup heavy cream

2 tablespoon milk

1 1/4 (6 oz) cups slivered almonds
very finely ground

1 1/2 cups flaked coconut

Directions:

1. Melt chocolate in microwave.
2. Stir in the almonds, heavy cream, and milk.
3. Pour mixture into an 8-inch square pan.
4. Chill, uncovered, until firm, about half an hour.
5. Cut into 32 squares.
6. Roll each square into a ball, and then roll in the coconut.
7. Chill the balls until ready to serve.

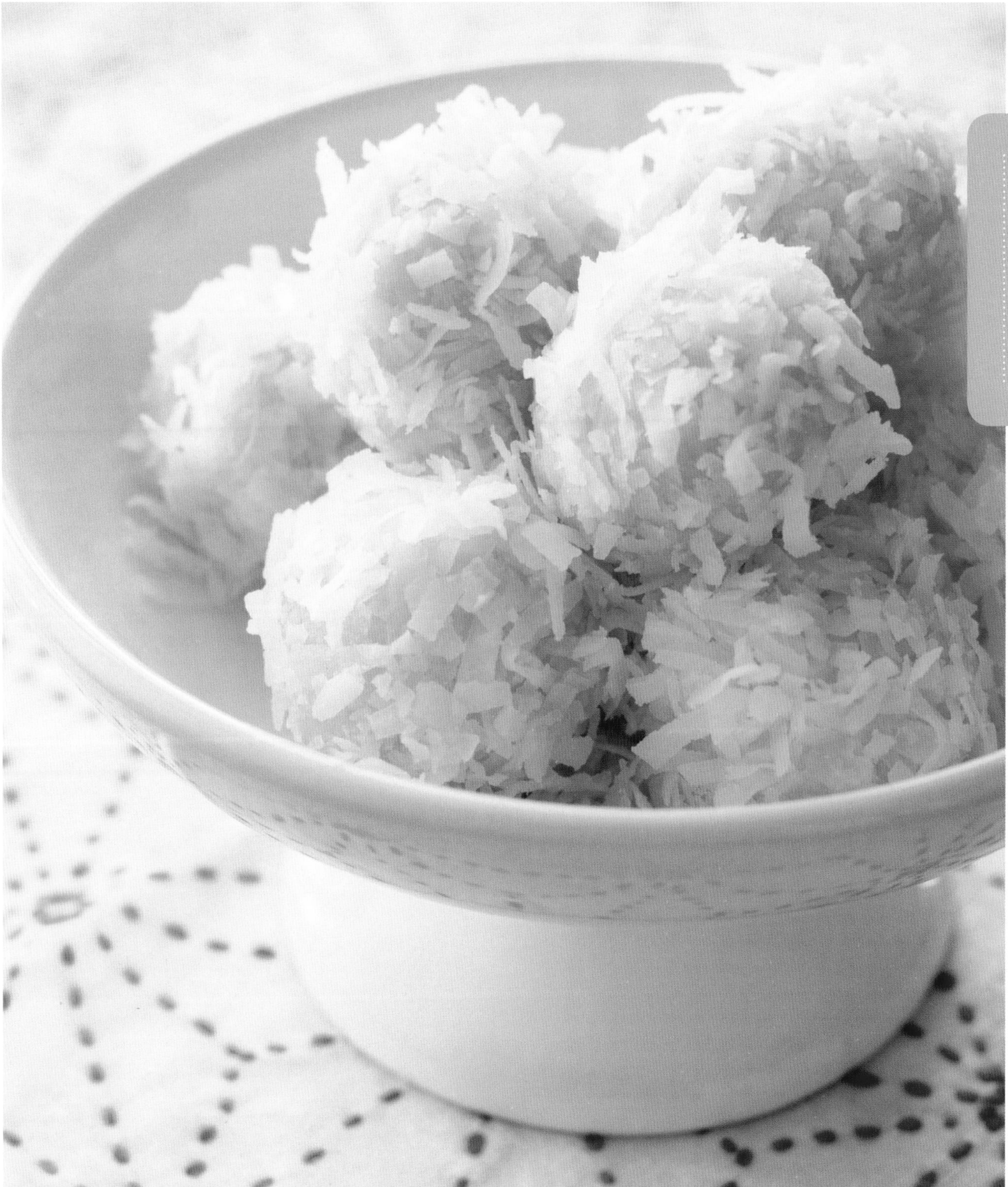

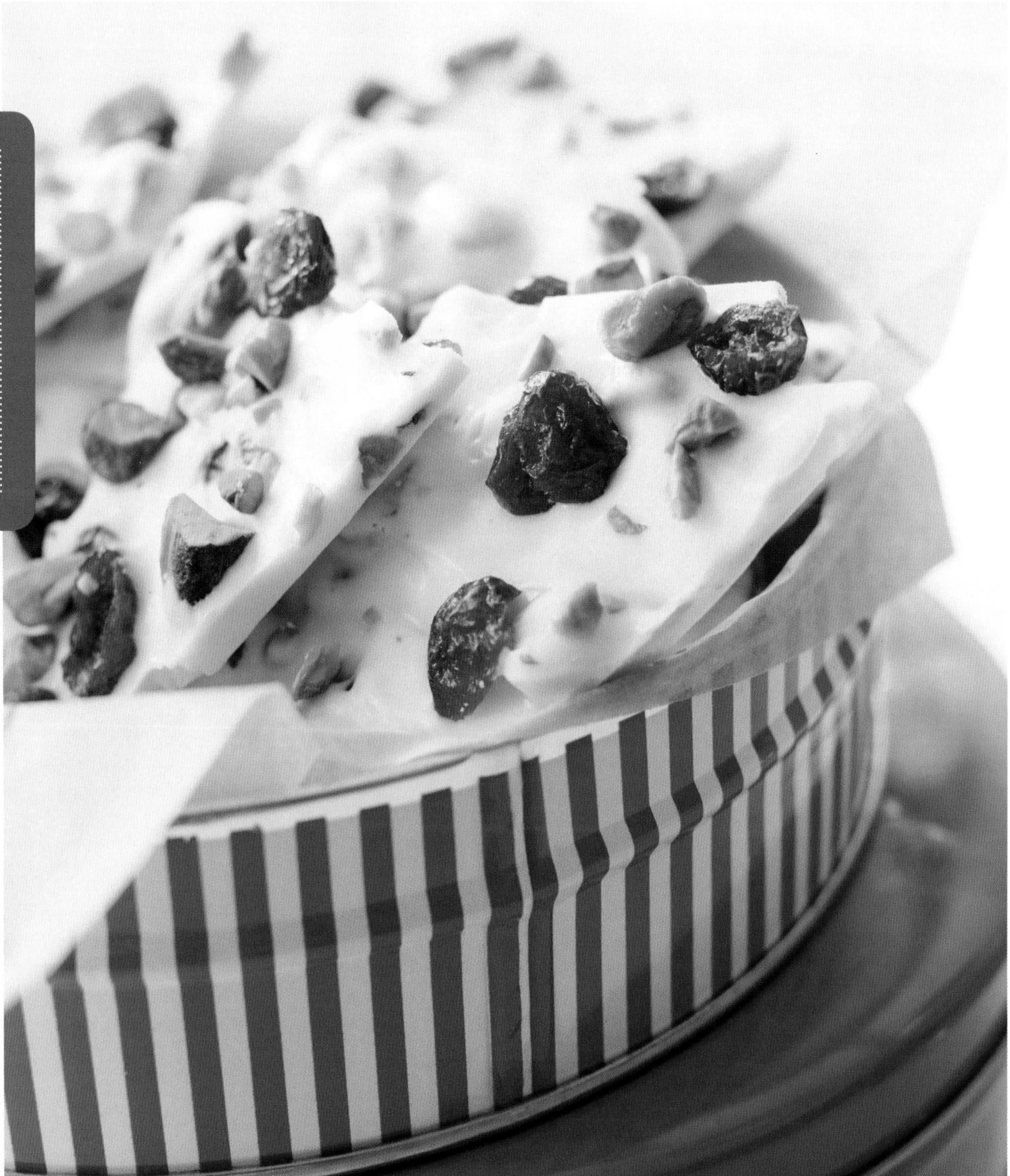

PISTACHIO CRANBERRY BARK

MAKES
2
POUNDS

This recipe works well for gift baskets, filling a festive bowl on your holiday table, or as a sweet treat with your coffee after dinner.

Ingredients:

1 (5 oz) cup coarsely chopped pistachios
1 cup (5 oz) dried cranberries
24 ounce semisweet chocolate or white chocolate chips

Directions:

1. Line a baking sheet with foil.
2. In a bowl, combine the pistachios and cranberries. Measure out half the mixture and set aside.
3. Melt the chocolate chips in the microwave.
4. Stir the pistachio-and-cranberry mixture into the chocolate mixture.
5. Spread the mixture evenly over the baking sheet.
6. Sprinkle the reserved pistachios and cranberries over the chocolate, and use a spatula to gently press them in.
7. Refrigerate for 30 minutes or until hardened.
8. Break into uneven pieces.

SUGAR COOKIES

MAKES
4
DOZEN

There are so many variations to this traditional, sweet and tender treat. Serve plain, or sprinkle granulated sugar on top for a more sophisticated look.

Ingredients:

3/4 cup (1 1/2 sticks) unsalted butter
1 cup sugar
2 large eggs
1/2 teaspoon vanilla extract
1/2 teaspoon almond extract
2 1/2 cups flour
1 teaspoon baking powder
1 teaspoon salt
Coarse sugar for sprinkling

Directions:

PART 1:

1. In a large bowl, and with an electric mixer, beat together the butter, sugar, eggs, and vanilla and almond extracts.
2. On a sheet of waxed paper, sift together the flour, baking powder, and salt.
3. Add the flour mixture to the butter mixture until it forms a dough.
4. Divide the dough in half, and pat into disks. Wrap in waxed paper and refrigerate overnight.

PART 2:

1. Preheat oven to 375°F.
2. Working with one piece of dough at a time, roll out 1/8 inch thick.
3. Cut into desired shapes with cookie cutters.
4. Gather the scraps, reroll, and cut more cookies.
5. Sprinkle the cookies with coarse sugar, and place on an ungreased baking sheet.
6. Bake for 6 to 10 minutes or until golden.

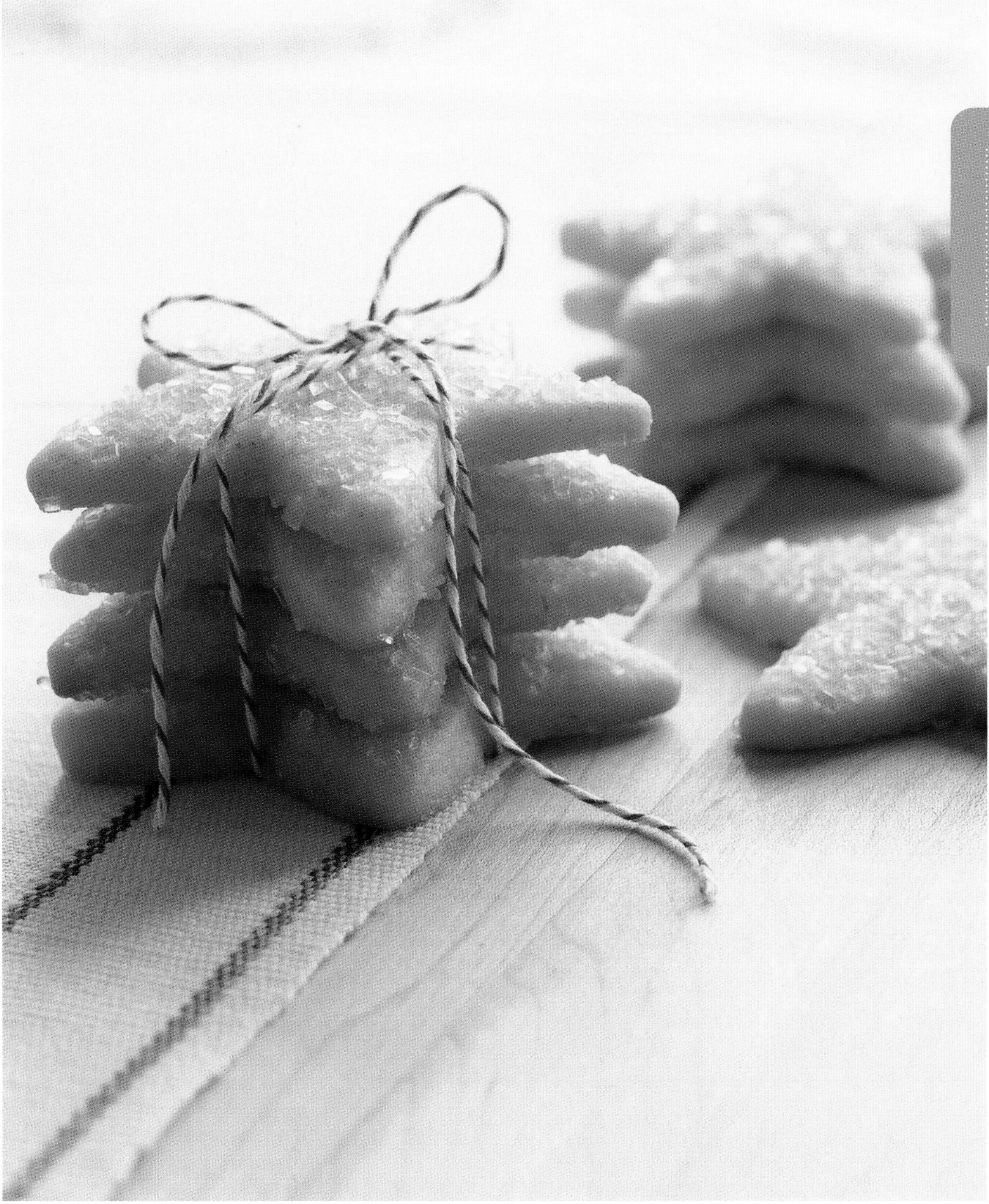

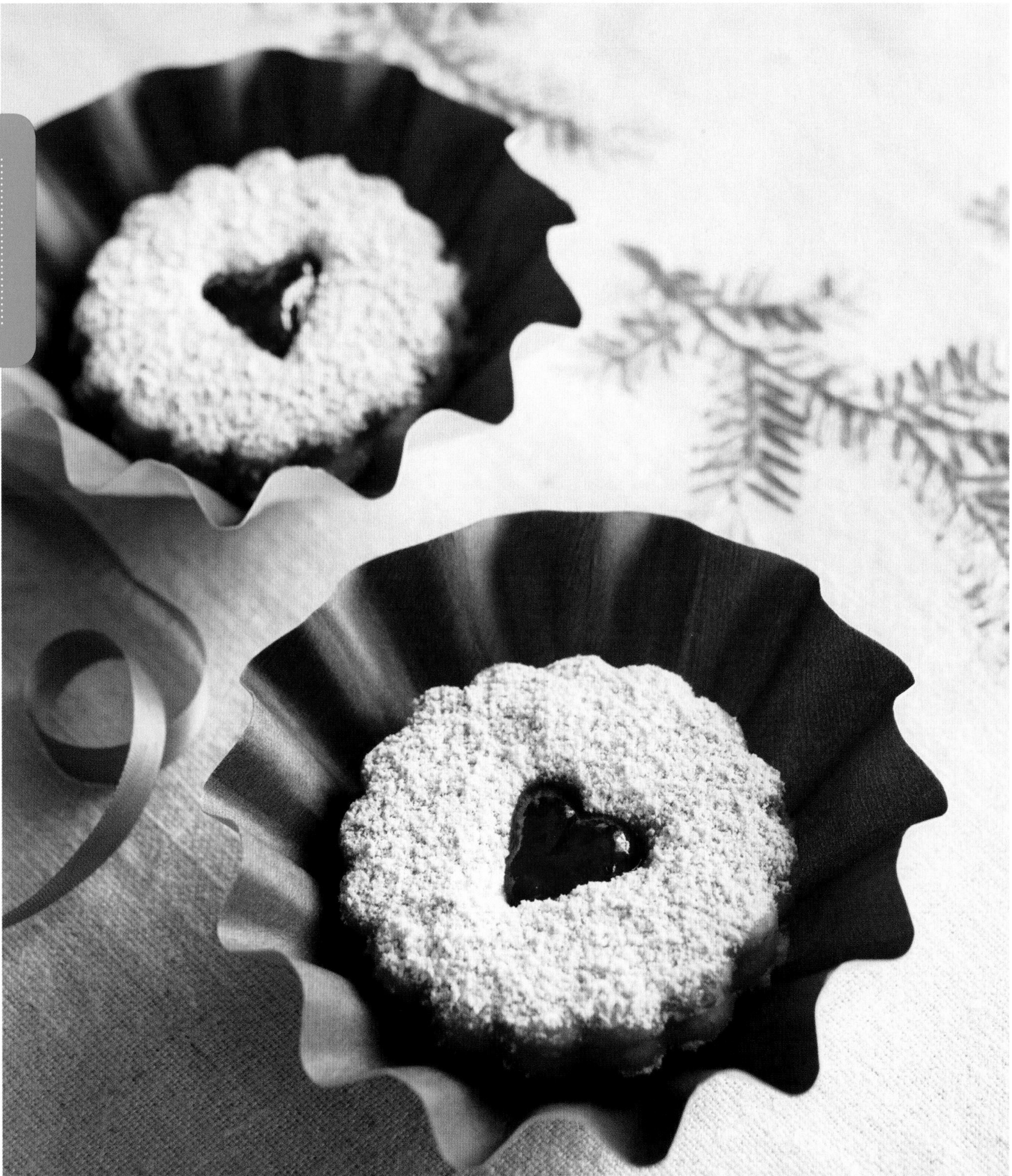

LINZER TARTS

MAKES
5
DOZEN

This Dutch cookie uses the same ingredients as the Linzertorte, but is presented in a different way. Use multiple cookie cutters for the center cutout to give your cookies some variety.

Ingredients:

1 1/2 cups (3 sticks) unsalted butter, (at room temperature)
1 3/4 cups confectioners' sugar
1 large egg
2 cups sifted flour
1 cup cornstarch
2 cups walnuts, finely ground
2/3 cup red raspberry jam

Directions:

PART 1:

1. In a large bowl, cream the butter and 1 cup confectioners' sugar until light & fluffy.
2. Add the egg and mix well.
3. Sift the flour and cornstarch together. Add to the butter mixture and blend well.
4. Mix in the walnuts.
5. Gather the dough into a ball, wrap in waxed paper or plastic wrap, and chill for 4 hours or overnight.

PART 2:

1. Preheat oven to 350°F.
2. On a lightly floured surface, roll the dough out 1/4 inch thick.
3. Using a 2-inch round cookie cutter, cut out cookies and place on an ungreased baking sheet.
4. Gather scraps, reroll, and cut out more cookies.
5. Chill the cookies for 15 minutes.
6. For half the cookies, cut out a small pattern from the middle.
7. Bake cookies for 13 to 15 minutes, until they are evenly and lightly browned.
8. Transfer to wire racks to cool.
9. Sift the remaining 3/4 cups confectioners' sugar into a bowl, and coat the cookies on one side.
10. Spread the jam on the nonsugared side.
11. Top each cookie with jam, with a cookie with the cutout center, sugared side out.

GERMAN CHOCOLATE-HAZELNUT WAFERS

MAKES
5
DOZEN

Shredded bittersweet chocolate and toasty hazelnuts intertwine in these crispy cookies. Stack the wafers and then wrap the cylinder in pretty paper for an easy-to-tote gift.

Ingredients:

1 cup toasted, skinned hazelnuts
or toasted almonds (page 15)
1/3 cup sugar
4 ounces bittersweet chocolate,
roughly chopped
1/2 cup unsalted butter,
(at room temperature)
1 teaspoon vanilla extract
2 teaspoons Frangelico or Amaretto
2 egg yolks
1 cup all-purpose flour

Directions:

PART 1:

1. In a food processor or blender, combine the nuts and 1 tablespoon of the sugar and grind finely.
2. Transfer to a bowl.
3. Place chocolate in the same appliance and process until finely shredded.
4. Add to the bowl holding the nuts.
5. In a bowl, using an electric mixer or a spoon, cream together the butter and the remaining sugar until light.
6. Beat in the vanilla, liqueur, and egg yolks until well mixed.
7. Add the flour and the reserved nuts and chocolate and mix until blended.
8. Scrape out onto a sheet of plastic wrap and, using the wrap, not your fingers, shape into a log about 2 1/4 inches in diameter.
9. Wrap and chill for 1 hour, or until firm.

PART 2:

1. Preheat the oven to 325°F.
2. Lightly grease baking sheets, or use nonstick baking sheets.
3. Slice the log into rounds 3/16 inch thick.
4. Place on the prepared baking sheets, spacing them about 1 1/2 inches apart.
5. One sheet at a time, bake the cookies for 10 to 12 minutes, or until light brown on the edges.
6. Transfer to racks to cool.

CHOCOLATE-SHEATHED ALMOND BISCOTTI

MAKES
4 1/2
DOZEN

A chocolate ribbon glazes these crispy, cinnamony biscotti. They make superb gifts, as they keep beautifully in a holiday cookie tin or slipped into a plastic bag and then packed in a festive paper gift sack.

Ingredients:

3 eggs

1 teaspoon vanilla extract

1/4 teaspoon almond extract

2 1/4 cups unbleached or all-purpose flour

3/4 cup plus 2 tablespoons sugar

1 teaspoon baking soda

1/2 teaspoon salt

2 teaspoons ground cinnamon

3/4 cup toasted raw almonds (page 15), chopped into halves or thirds

CHOCOLATE GLAZE:

6 ounces bittersweet chocolate

1/2 teaspoon vegetable shortening

Directions:

1. Preheat the oven to 325°F.
2. Grease and flour a baking sheet.
3. In a small bowl, using a whisk, beat together the eggs and the vanilla and almond extracts until blended.
4. In a large bowl, stir together the flour, sugar, baking soda, salt, and cinnamon.
5. Add the egg mixture to the flour mixture and mix with an electric mixer or a spoon until blended.
6. Stir in the nuts.
7. Divide the dough in half.
8. One at a time, place the 2 dough portions on the prepared baking sheet and form each into a log about 1/2 inch high, 1 1/2 inches wide, and 14 inches long.
9. Space the logs at least 2 inches apart.
10. Bake the logs for 25 minutes, or until set and golden brown.
11. Transfer to a rack and let cool on the baking sheet for 6 to 8 minutes.
12. Reduce the oven temperature to 300°F.
13. Transfer the logs to a cutting board.
14. Using a serrated knife, slice at a 45-degree angle about 3/8 inch thick.
15. Lay the slices flat on the baking sheet and return to the oven for 15 minutes longer, turning them once, to dry slightly.
16. Transfer to racks to cool.

FOR THE GLAZE:

1. In the top pan of a double boiler, combine the chocolate and shortening.
2. Place over hot water in the lower pan and heat until melted, then stir until smooth.
3. Using an icing spatula, spread the chocolate over the top surface of the cookies.
4. Let cool until set.

ALMOND SHORTBREAD SNOWFLAKES

MAKES
15
COOKIES

To give these cookies even more almond flavor, substitute half a cup almond flour for the all-purpose flour in the batter.

Ingredients:

1 cup butter
(at room temperature)
1/2 cup granulated sugar
1 tablespoon almond extract
2 1/2 cups of all-purpose flour

Directions:

1. Preheat oven to 350°F.
2. Cream butter and sugar together.
3. Mix in extract and flour.
4. With a rolling pin, on a lightly floured surface, roll dough out to approximately 3/4 inch thickness.
5. Cut with floured snowflake 2 1/2-inch cookie cutter.
6. Place cookies on ungreased cookie sheet.
7. Bake at 350°F for 10 to 12 minutes or until cookies are golden brown on top.
8. Remove cookies from cookie sheet; cool.

FOR ADDED FUN:

1. Melt 4 oz of white chocolate or almond bark in a microwave.
2. Dip cookies in white chocolate or almond bark.
3. Place on waxed paper to dry.
4. Sprinkle cookies with coarse sugar while the chocolate or almond bark is still wet to add sparkle.

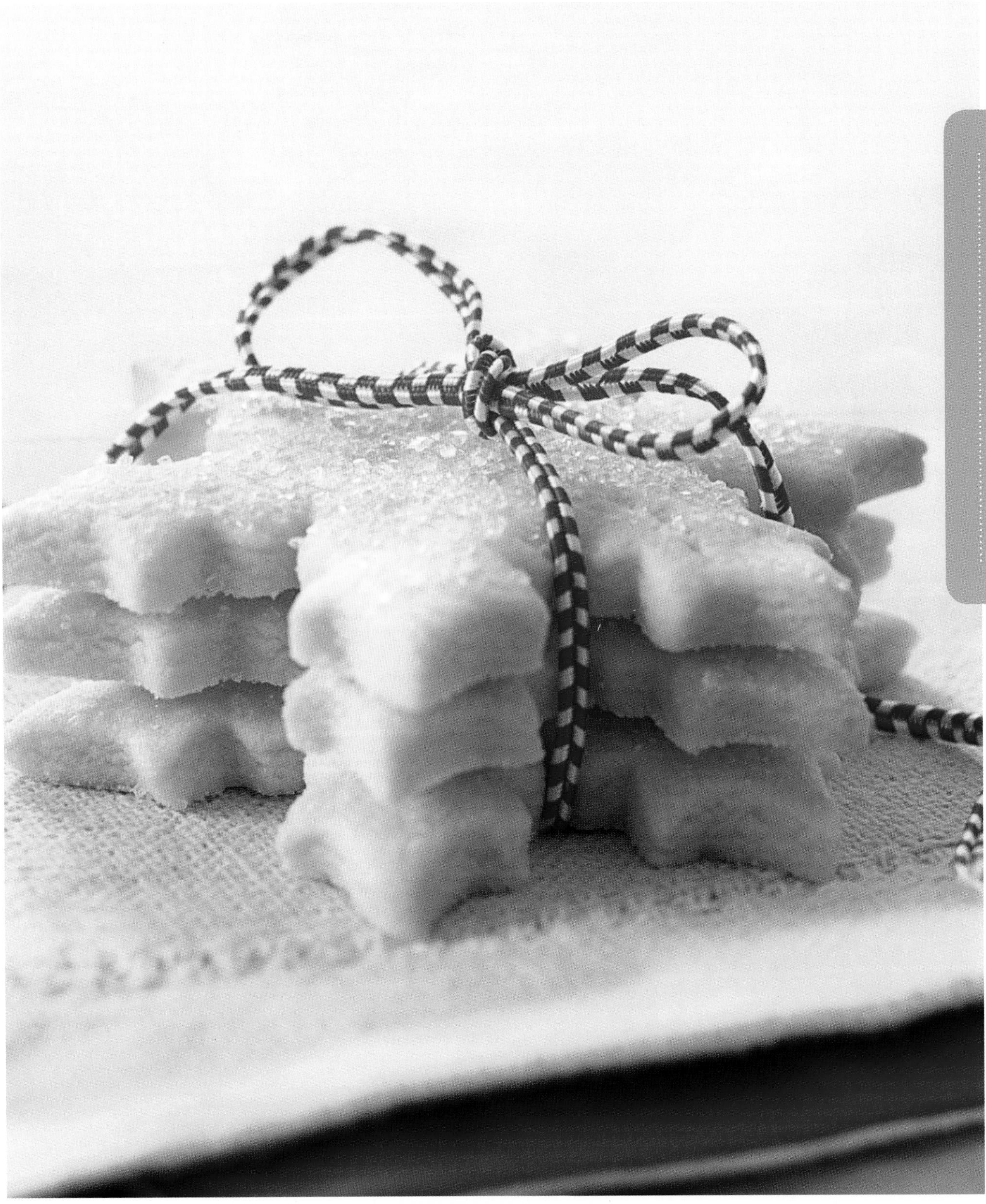

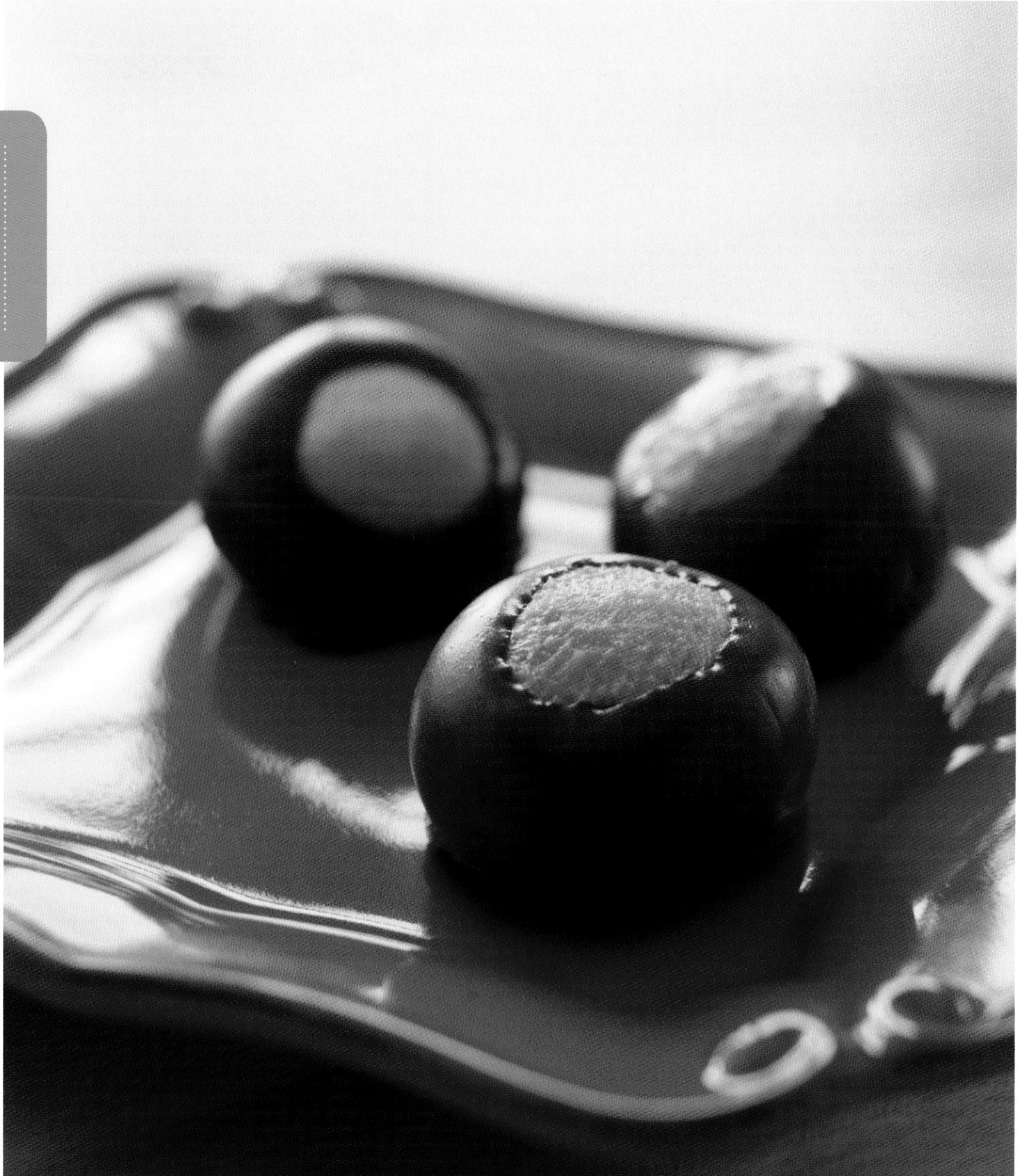

BUCKEYE BALLS

MAKES
80
COOKIES

Leave a small portion of the peanut butter showing at the top of these ball cookies to give them the appearance of buckeyes, the nut these cookies are named for.

Ingredients:

1 18-ounce jar of creamy peanut butter
1 cup (2 sticks) butter
(at room temperature)
1 pound confectioners' sugar
2 cups (8 oz) graham cracker crumbs
24 ounce semisweet chocolate chips
4 tablespoons shortening

Directions:

1. In a medium bowl, with an electric mixer, blend the peanut butter and butter until soft and creamy.
2. Beat in the confectioners' sugar.
3. Stir in the graham cracker crumbs.
4. Using a heaping teaspoon of the mixture, roll into balls.
5. Place the balls on a tray, and chill in the freezer for 15 minutes.
6. Melt chocolate chips and shortening in the microwave. Stir well to blend.
7. Line a cookie sheet with foil, and spray lightly with nonstick cooking spray.
8. Spear a scat ball with a toothpick, and dip into the chocolate to cover the ball.
9. Place on the foil. Chill to set the chocolate coating.

CHOCOLATE CRINKLES

MAKES
5
DOZEN

This cookie is crunchy on the outside, but soft and chewy on the inside. It has an attractive light and dark contrast, making a perfect addition to any cookie tray.

Ingredients:

4 ounces unsweetened chocolate

1/4 cup vegetable oil

2 cups granulated sugar

4 large eggs

2 teaspoon vanilla extract

2 cups flour

2 teaspoon baking powder

1/2 teaspoon salt

1 cup confectioners' sugar

Directions:

PART 1:

1. Melt chocolate in microwave.
2. In a large bowl, with an electric mixer, blend together the oil and granulated sugar. Add the eggs one at a time, beating well after each addition. Beat in the melted chocolate and vanilla.
3. In a separate bowl, whisk together the flour, baking powder, and salt.
4. Add the flour mixture to the chocolate mixture gradually. Mix until well combined (the dough will be stiff).
5. Chill overnight or until the dough is firm enough to be rolled into balls.

PART 2:

1. Preheat oven to 350°F.
2. Line a baking sheet with a nonstick liner or parchment paper.
3. Roll the dough into 1-inch balls, and roll them in confectioners' sugar.
4. Place on the baking sheet about 1 inch apart. Bake for 10 to 13 minutes (take them out after 10 minutes if you want them soft and gooey).
5. Let cool for 2 minutes on the baking sheet; then transfer to a wire rack to cool completely.

WHITE CHOCOLATE CRANBERRY COOKIES

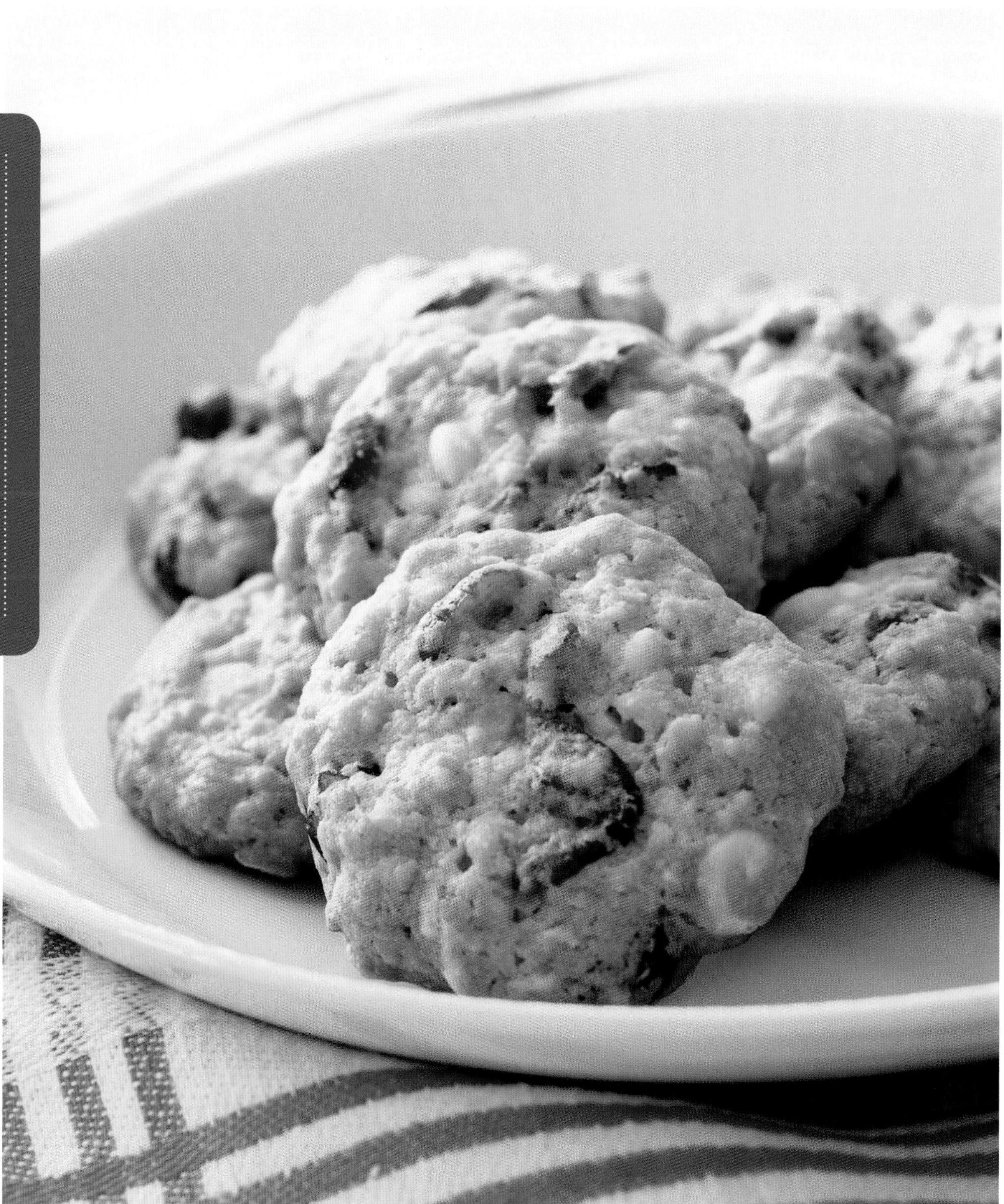

WHITE CHOCOLATE CRANBERRY COOKIES

MAKES
5-6
DOZEN

These cookies boast a yummy sweetness fit for any party. For an extra holiday kick, substitute a teaspoon of brandy for the vanilla.

Ingredients:

2 cups old-fashioned rolled oats
2 cups flour
3/4 teaspoon baking soda
1/2 teaspoon baking powder
1/2 teaspoon salt
1/4 teaspoon cinnamon
1 cup (2 sticks) unsalted butter,
(at room temperature)
1 cup packed light brown sugar
2 eggs, room temperature
1 tsp vanilla extract
1-12 ounce pkg white chocolate chips
1 cup dried, sweetened cranberries

Directions:

1. In a large bowl, stir together the oats, flour, baking soda, baking powder, salt, and cinnamon.
2. In a separate bowl, blend the butter and sugar with an electric mixer until smooth.
3. Add the eggs and continue to beat until fluffy.
4. Blend in vanilla extract.
5. Using a wooden spoon, stir the dry mixture into the butter mixture one half at a time. Mix in the white chocolate chips and cranberries.
6. Refrigerate the dough for 1 to 2 hours.
7. Preheat the oven to 375°F.
8. Line a large baking sheet with greased aluminum foil.
9. Shape the dough into 1-inch balls, and place them on foil about 2 1/2-3 inches apart.
10. Use your fingertips to flatten each ball to 1/3 inch thick.
11. Bake the cookies on the center oven rack for 10 to 12 minutes, turning the sheet about halfway through. When they're done, the cookies should be very lightly browned and still look moist.
12. Cool the cookies on the baking sheet for 3 minutes; then transfer them to a wire rack.

MOLASSES SUGAR COOKIES

MAKES
4
DOZEN

Molasses gives these cookies their signature dark ginger brown color, adds to their sweet flavor, and gives them that moist and soft texture. For added fun, place one scoop of vanilla icea cream between two cookies for a delectable dessert.

Ingredients:

3/4 cup shortening
1 cup sugar
1/4 cup molasses
1 egg
2 teaspoon baking soda
2 cups sifted all-purpose flour
1/2 teaspoon cloves
1/2 teaspoon ginger
1 teaspoon cinnamon
1/2 teaspoon salt
Granulated sugar (for coating)

Directions:

PART 1:

1. Melt shortening in a 3 or 4-quart saucepan over low heat.
2. Remove from heat; let cool.
3. Add sugar, molasses, and egg. Beat well.
4. Sift together flour, baking soda, cloves, cinnamon, ginger, and salt.
5. Add to 1st mixture. Mix well.
6. Chill for at least 30 minutes.

PART 2:

1. Preheat oven to 375°F.
2. Form into 1-inch balls.
3. Roll in granulated sugar, and place on lightly greased cookie sheets, 2 inches apart.
4. Bake for 8 to 10 minutes.

OATMEAL COOKIES

MAKES
6
DOZEN

For a superior flavor and richer textured cookie, make sure to use old-fashioned rolled oats for this recipe instead of quick-cooking. To make the recipe more kid-friendly, feel free to add chocolate chips to the batter.

Ingredients:

1 1/2 cups (3 sticks) unsalted butter,
(at room temperature)

1 cup packed light brown sugar

1 cup granulated sugar

1 large egg

1 1/2 teaspoon vanilla extract

3 cups old-fashioned rolled oats

1 1/2 cups flour

2 1/2 teaspoon baking soda

3/4 teaspoon salt

1 1/2 cups dried cranberries
(may substitute raisins)

Directions:

1. Preheat the oven to 350°F.
2. Line a baking sheet with parchment paper.
3. In a large bowl, with an electric mixer, blend together the butter, brown sugar, and granulated sugar.
4. Mix in the egg and vanilla.
5. Stir in the oats, flour, baking soda, salt, and cranberries.
6. Drop the dough by rounded teaspoon onto the baking sheet about 2 inches apart.
7. Bake for 8 to 10 minutes, or until lightly browned around the edges.
8. Let cool on the baking sheet for 2 minutes before transferring to a wire rack to cool completely.

DOUBLE CRUNCHERS

MAKES
3
DOZEN

This recipe has withstood the test of time, using cornflakes and old-fashioned oats in the cookie batter, as well as melted chocolate chips and sugar for the center. The result? Two cookies sandwiching a fudgy center making twice the treat!

Ingredients:

1 cup flour

1/2 teaspoon baking soda

1/4 teaspoon salt

1/2 cup solid vegetable
shortening

1/2 cup packed light
brown sugar

1/2 cup granulated sugar

1 large egg

1/2 teaspoon vanilla extract

1 cup cornflakes, crushed

1 cup old-fashioned rolled oats

1/2 cup shredded coconut

1 package (6 oz) semisweet
chocolate chips

1/2 cup confectioners' sugar

1 tablespoon water

3 ounces cream cheese,
(at room temperature)

Directions:

1. Preheat oven to 350°F.
2. Sift together the flour, baking soda, and salt.
3. In a medium bowl, with an electric mixer, cream together the shortening, brown sugar, and granulated sugar until light and creamy.
4. Add the egg and vanilla and beat well.
5. Add the flour mixture.
6. Blend in the cornflakes, oats, and coconut.
7. Divide the dough into two pieces, one twice as large as the other.
8. Shape the larger into balls about 3/4 inches in diameter.
9. Shape the small piece into the same number of balls (they will be smaller).
10. Place the balls on a lined baking sheet, and flatten them to a 1/4 inch thickness.
11. Bake for 9 to 12 minutes, until golden.
12. Let sit on the baking sheet for 5 minutes. Transfer to rack to cool.
13. Meanwhile, make the frosting: Melt together the chocolate chips, confectioners' sugar, and water in the microwave.
14. Beat in the cream cheese.
15. Frost the larger cookie and top with the smaller ones.

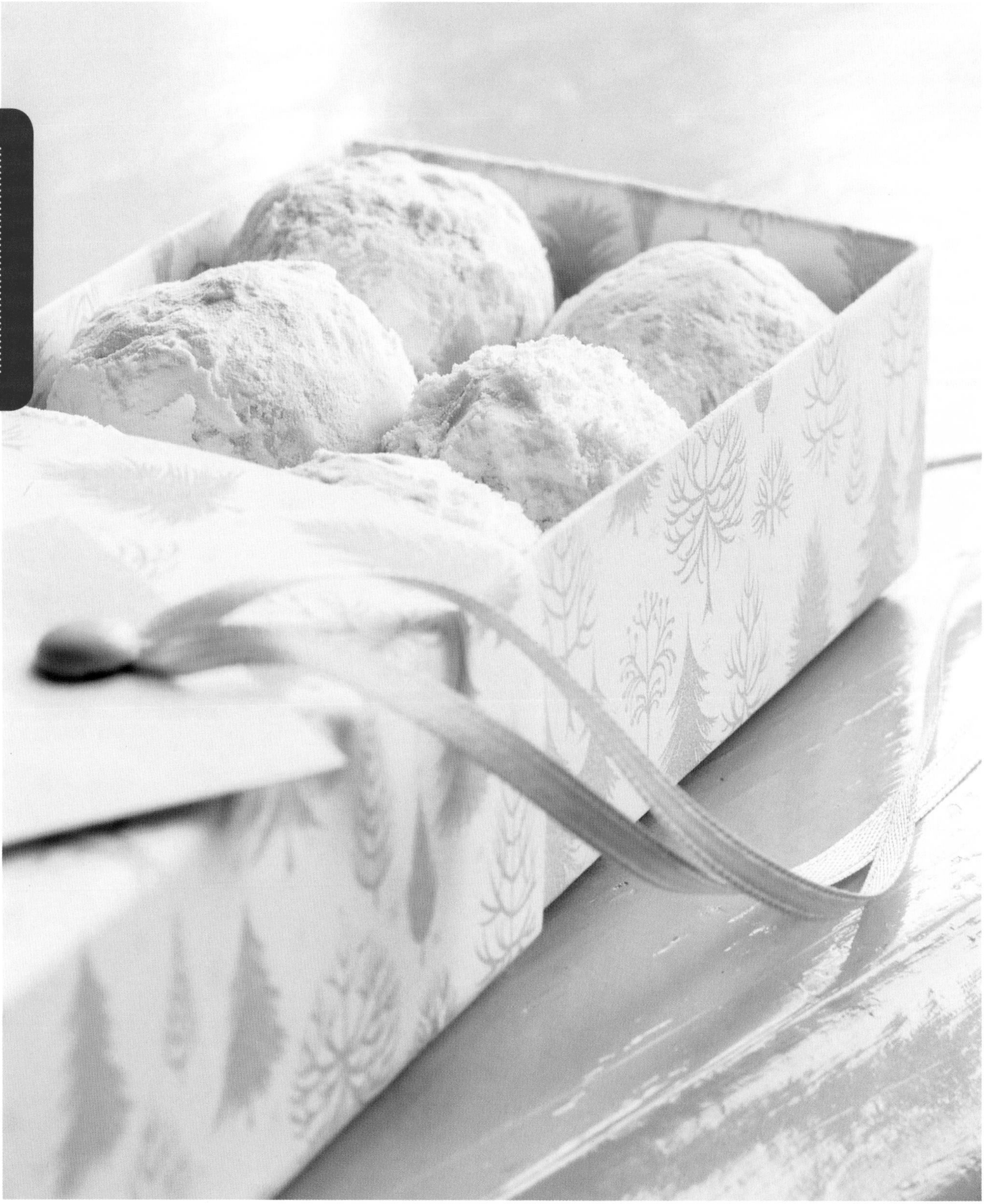

RUSSIAN TEA CAKES

MAKES
3
DOZEN

These cookies have been known by many names, including Mexican Wedding Cakes and Italian Butternuts. The recipe itself dates back to the 18th century. Why mess with perfection?

Ingredients:

1 cup (2 sticks) unsalted butter
(at room temperature)
1/2 cup confectioners' sugar
1 teaspoon vanilla extract
2 1/4 cups flour
Pinch of salt
3/4 cup chopped pecans
Confectioners' sugar, for coating

Directions:

PART 1:
1. In a large bowl, with an electric mixer, beat the butter and the confectioners' sugar until creamy.
2. Beat in vanilla.
3. Gradually add the flour and salt and beat until combined.
4. Stir in pecans.
5. Cover and refrigerate for at least one hour or overnight.

PART 2:
1. Preheat oven to 350°F.
2. Shape the dough into 1-inch balls, and place on an ungreased baking sheet.
3. Bake for 12 to 14 minutes, until nicely browned.
4. Transfer to wire racks.
5. Coat the cool cookies in confectioners' sugar.

PUMPERNICKEL COOKIES

MAKES
6
DOZEN

The word "pumpernickel" originally referred to a type of dark rye bread of German Westphalian origin. The original pumpernickel was made with coarsely crushed whole rye and water only, without using sweetening agents, flours, or other ingredients. These cookies, however, are made with flour and hazelnuts, raisins, and citrus zest for a slight sweet flavor.

Ingredients:

1/2 cup (1 stick) unsalted butter
(at room temperature)
1 cup sugar
4 large eggs plus 1 egg,
lightly beaten, for egg wash
4 cups flour
1 teaspoon baking soda
Grated zest of lemon
Grated zest of orange
1/2 cup chopped skinned hazelnuts
3/4 cup golden raisins

Directions:

1. Preheat oven to 350°F.
2. Grease 2 baking sheets.
3. In a large bowl, with an electric mixer, beat the butter and gradually add the sugar.
4. Add the 4 eggs, one at a time, beating well after each addition.
5. On a sheet of waxed paper, sift the flour and baking soda together.
6. Gradually add the flour mixture to the butter mixture.
7. Stir in the grated zests, hazelnuts, and raisins.
8. Using floured hands, divide the dough into eight pieces. Roll each piece into a rope about 12 inches long.
9. Place four ropes on each of the baking sheets and press lightly to flatten.
10. Brush with egg wash.
11. Bake for 15 to 20 minutes, until light golden brown.
12. While still hot, cut on the diagonal into 1 1/2 inch pieces.
13. Scatter around the baking sheet, and return to the oven for 2 min.
14. Transfer to wire racks to cool.

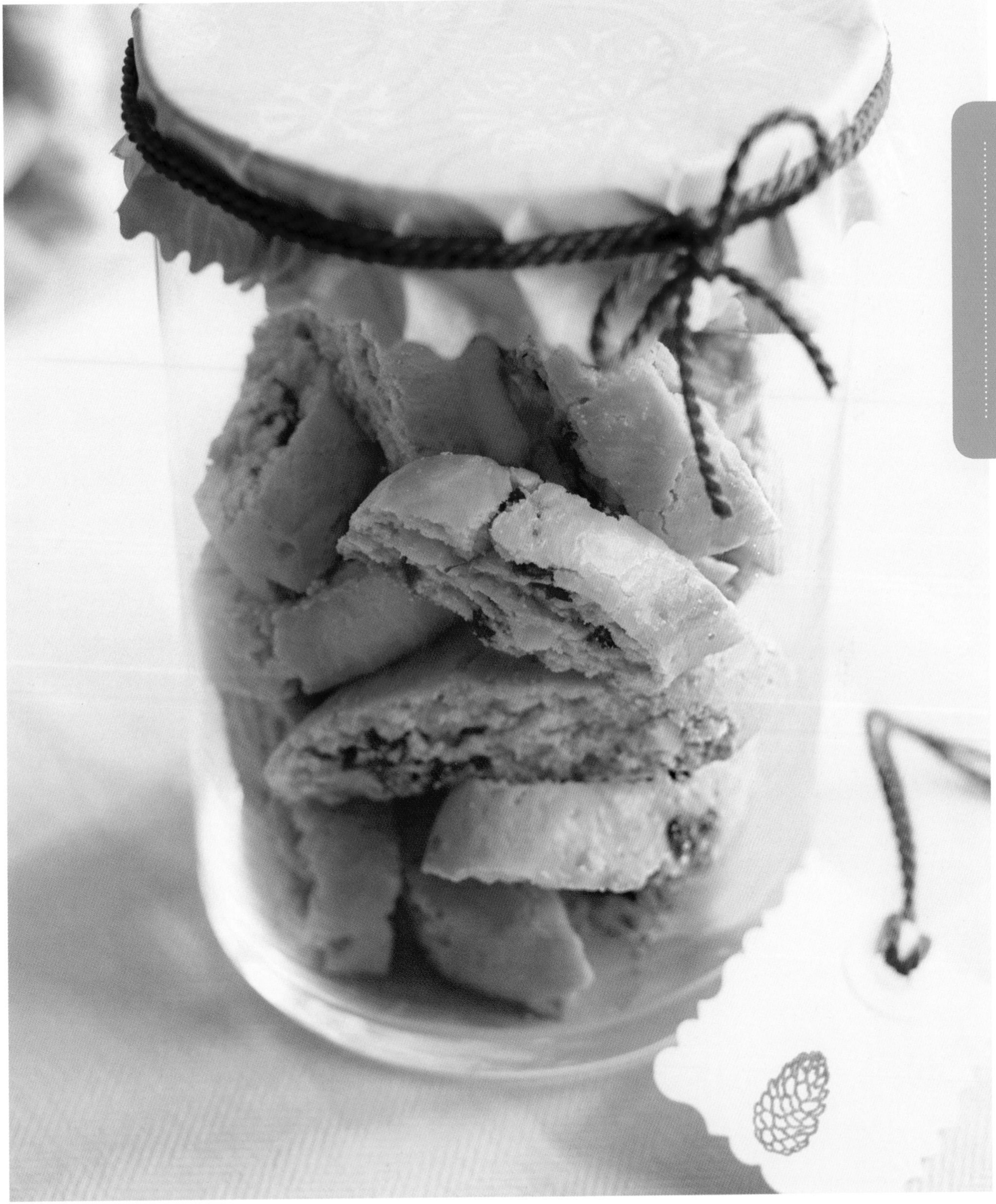

CHERRY-HAZELNUT CHOCOLATE CHIP COOKIES

MAKES
2 1/2
DOZEN

Dried cherries lend a holiday sparkle and sweet-tart flavor to the classic chocolate chip cookie, a favorite on any cookie tray. It is easy to adapt the recipe to other nuts, dried fruits, and chocolate, such as white chocolate chips and macadamia nuts or golden raisins and pistachios.

Ingredients:

1/2 cup unsalted butter
(at room temperature)
1/2 cup granulated sugar
1/4 cup firmly packed dark
brown sugar
1/2 teaspoon vanilla extract
1 egg
1 cup plus 2 tablespoons
all-purpose flour
1/2 teaspoon baking soda
1/4 teaspoon salt
1 cup (6 ounces) double or
semisweet chocolate chips or
white chocolate chips
2/3 cup dried cherries
3/4 cup chopped toasted, skinned
hazelnuts (page 15) or chopped
walnuts, pecans, or macadamia nuts

Directions:

1. Preheat the oven to 375°F.
2. Lightly grease baking sheets, or use nonstick baking sheets.
3. In a large bowl, using an electric mixer or a spoon, cream together the butter and sugars until light.
4. Mix in the vanilla and egg until well blended.
5. In another bowl, stir together the flour, baking soda, and salt.
6. Add the flour mixture to the butter mixture and mix until blended.
7. Stir in the chocolate chips, cherries, and nuts.
8. Using a small scoop, drop mounds of the dough onto the prepared baking sheets, spacing them about 2 inches apart.
9. One sheet at a time, bake the cookies for 10 to 12 minutes, or until golden brown.
10. Transfer to racks to cool.

SWIRLED PEANUT BUTTER BARS

MAKES
3
DOZEN

The chocolate melts to form a decorative swirl
with the peanut butter topping.

Ingredients:

1/2 cup unsalted butter
(at room temperature)
1/2 cup granulated sugar
1/2 cup firmly packed dark
brown sugar
1 egg
1/3 cup smooth peanut butter
1 cup all-purpose flour
1 cup quick-cooking (not instant)
rolled oats
1/2 teaspoon baking soda
1/4 teaspoon salt

PEANUT BUTTER ICING:
1 cup powdered sugar
1/2 cup smooth peanut butter
3 to 4 tablespoons heavy cream
12 ounces semisweet chocolate chips
or bittersweet chocolate or milk
chocolate bars, chopped

Directions:

1. Preheat the oven to 350°F.
2. Lightly grease a 9-by-13-inch baking pan.
3. In a large bowl, using an electric mixer or a spoon,
   cream together the butter and sugars until light.
4. Add the egg and peanut butter and mix until blended.
5. In another bowl, stir together the flour, oats, baking soda, and salt.
6. Add the flour mixture to the butter mixture and mix until
   well blended.
7. Pat into the prepared pan.
8. Bake for 20 to 25 minutes, or until golden brown.
9. Meanwhile, make the icing: In a bowl, using a spoon, stir together
   the sugar, peanut butter, and enough heavy cream to form a
   mixture that can be drizzled.
10. When the baked bars are ready, remove from the oven and immediately
    sprinkle with the chocolate chips or chopped chocolate bars.
11. Let stand for 1 to 2 minutes to melt.
12. Drizzle the peanut mixture over the melting chocolate and, using an
    icing spatula, swirl together the chocolate and the topping.
13. Let cool in the pan on a rack.
14. Turn out of the pan and cut into 1 1/2-by-2-inch bars.

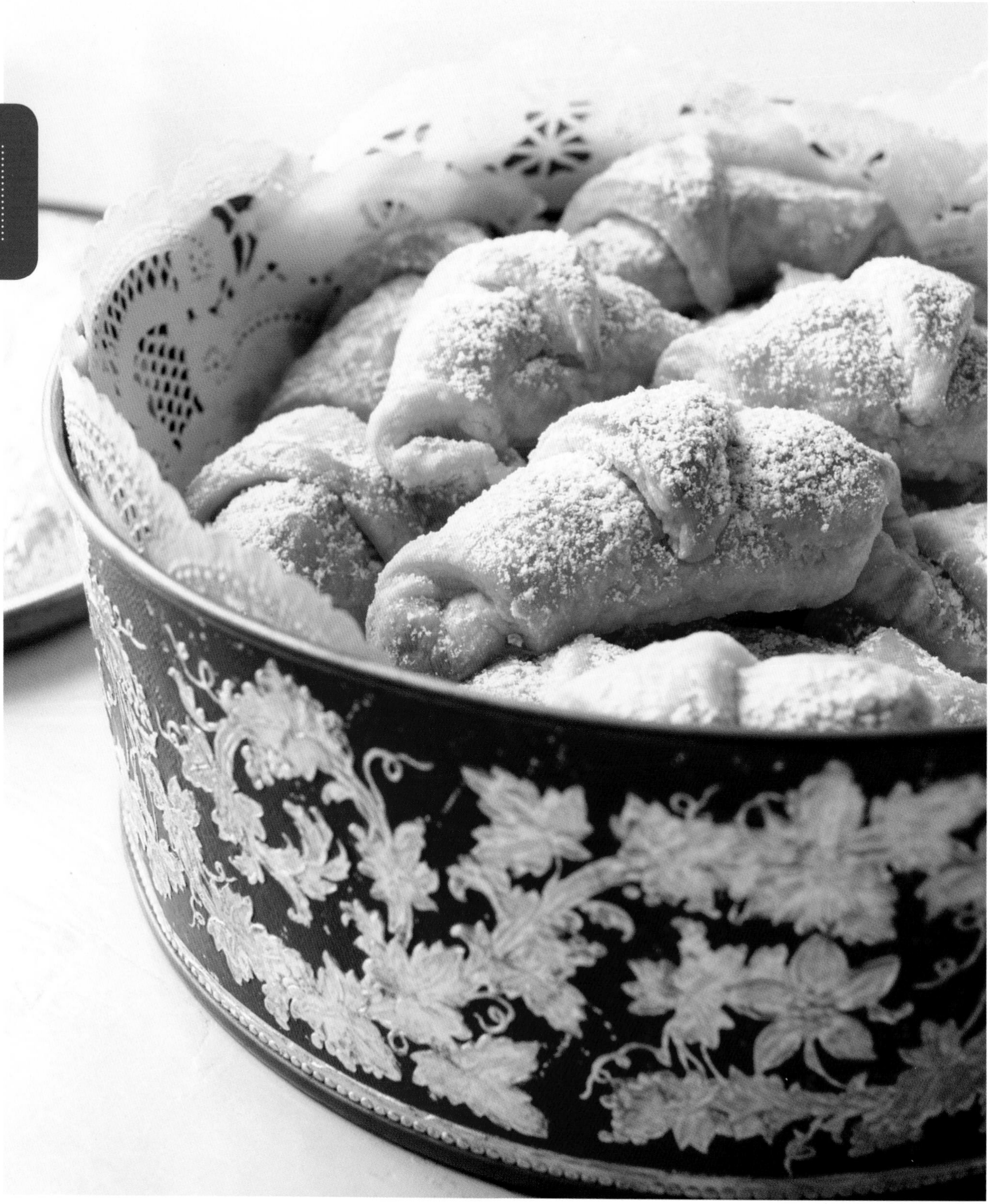

KIPFELS

MAKES 5 DOZEN

The word kipfel means "crescent," like its signature shape, and is the ancestor of the croissant. There is much folklore surrounding this cookie and its creation, but all stories agree that this Austrian cookie was created to celebrate victory in war.

Ingredients:

3 1/2 cups flour
2 cups (4 sticks) butter,
(at room temperature, cut into Tbsps)
1 pound cream cheese,
(at room temperature, cut into chunks)
1 teaspoon vanilla
1 teaspoon salt
1 teaspoon baking power
3/4 cup fruit spread or preserves
1 egg, lightly beaten, for egg wash
Confectioners' sugar, for dusting

Directions:

PART 1

1. In a large bowl, blend the flour and butter.
2. In another bowl, blend the cream cheese, vanilla, salt, and baking powder.
3. Add the cream cheese mixture to the butter mixture.
4. Divide the dough in half, wrap in waxed paper, and refrigerate for 1 hour or overnight.

PART 2

1. Preheat oven to 350°F.
2. Working with one half at a time, divide the dough into five pieces.
3. On a lightly floured surface, roll each piece into a 6-inch circle.
4. Cut into 6 wedges.
5. Drop about 1/2 teaspoon of the fruit spread, starting at the wide end and roll up.
6. Place on an ungreased baking sheet, and curve the end of the cookie inward to form a crescent.
7. Brush with the egg wash.
8. Bake for 16 to 17 minutes, until just golden.
9. Transfer to wire racks to cool.
10. Dust with confectioners' sugar before serving.

CHOCOLATE-PECAN RUM BALLS

MAKES
3 1/2
DOZEN

These truffle-like confections are sweet and dense balls flavored with chocolate and rum. Unlike most cookies, these are not baked, allowing the alcohol to add extra flavor and kick. For variety, you can substitute brandy for rum. Or, for a more kid-friendly snack, you can use rum extract.

Ingredients:

1 box (9 oz) chocolate wafer cookies, finely crushed

2 1/4 cups (8 oz) very finely chopped pecans

1 1/2 cups confectioners' sugar

2 to 5 tablespoons unsweetened cocoa powder

1/4 teaspoon salt

2 tablespoons light corn syrup

6 tablespoons dark rum
(for a more kid-friendly treat, substitute with rum extract)

3/4 cup granulated sugar

Directions:

1. In a large bowl, combine the cookie crumbs, pecans, confectioners' sugar, 2 Tbsp cocoa, and the salt.
2. Stir in the corn syrup and rum extract. Mix with your hands. The mixture should stick together easily but not be too sticky (add 2 to 3 tablespoons more cocoa if needed).
3. Form 1-inch balls and roll the balls in the granulated sugar.
4. Let stand at room temperature overnight. Store in an airtight container.

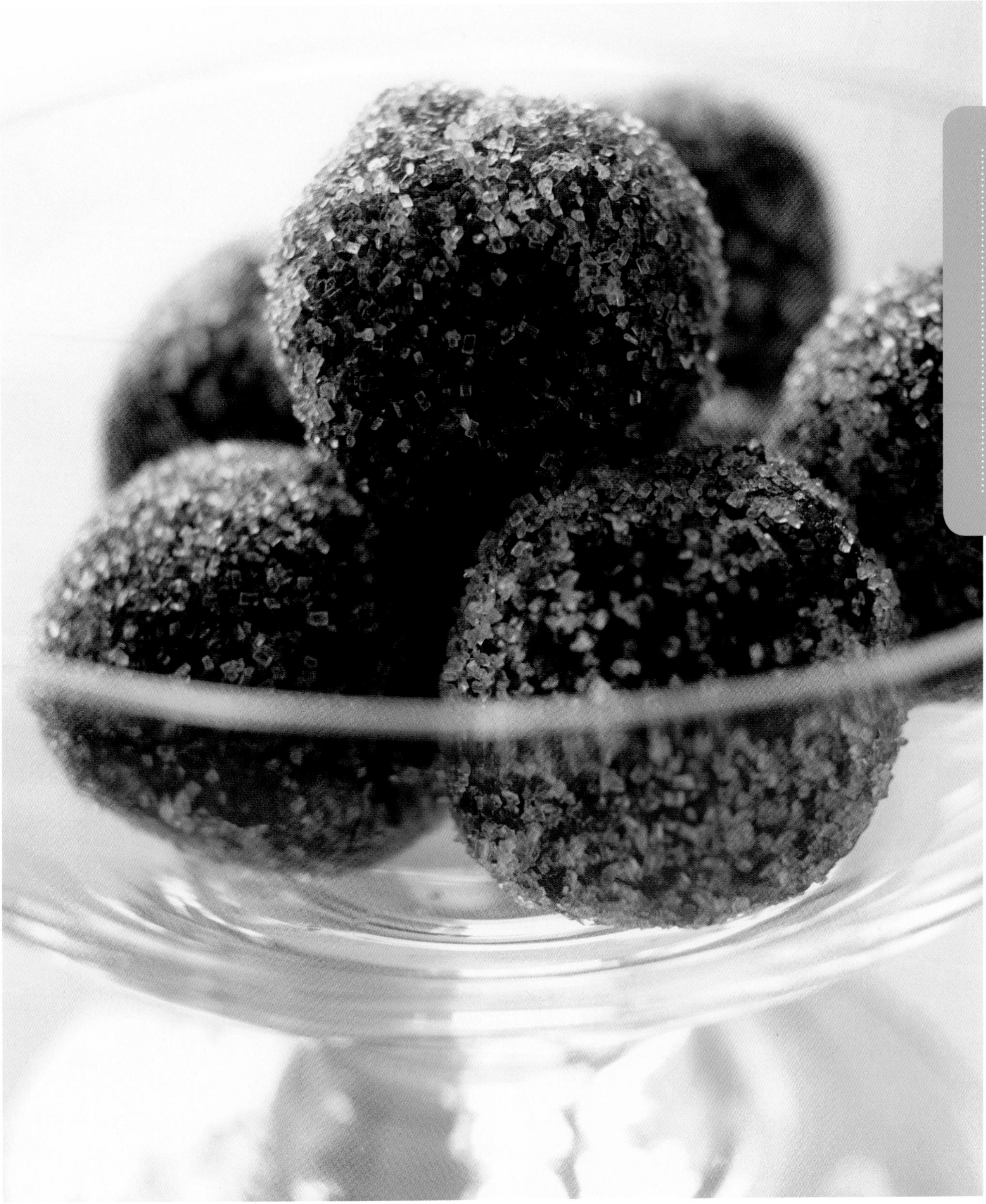

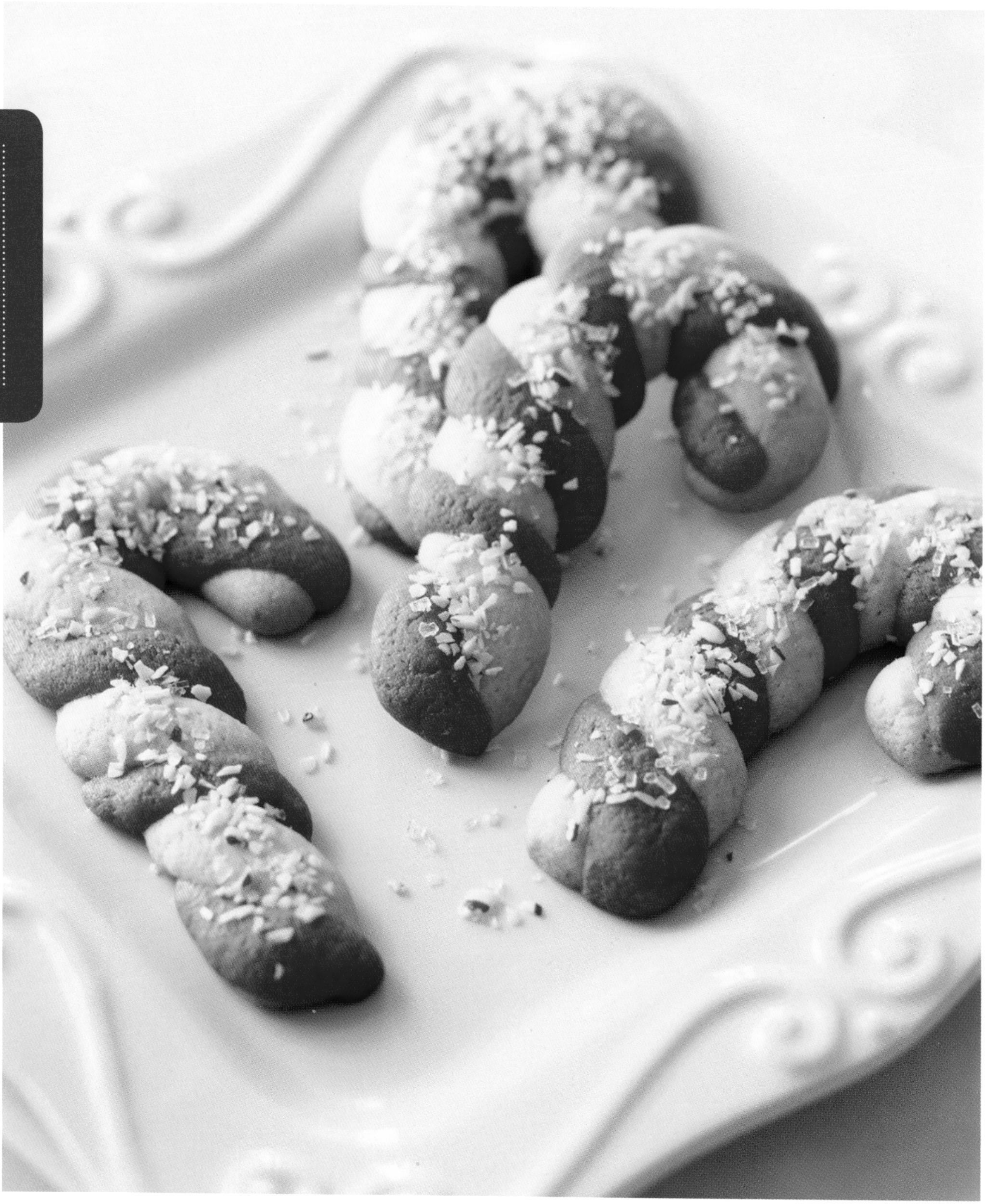

CANDY CANE COOKIES

MAKES
4
DOZEN

This is a simple yet fun way to celebrate the classic candy cane. Originally a straight peppermint stick, it is rumored that a choirmaster from Cologne Cathedral of Germany bent the peppermint sticks so they resembled a shepherd's crook and handed them out to the children at holiday mass.

Ingredients:

1 cup sugar

3/4 cup margarine or butter
(at room temperature)

2 eggs

1 1/2 teaspoons peppermint extract

2 1/2 cups all-purpose flour

1 teaspoon baking powder

1 teaspoon salt

1/2 teaspoon red food coloring

1/2 cup crushed peppermint candy

1/2 cup granulated sugar
(for sprinkling)

Directions:

PART 1

1. Mix sugar, butter, eggs, and peppermint extract.
2. Stir in flour, baking powder, and salt.
3. Divide dough into halves.
4. Tint one half with food coloring.
5. Cover and refrigerate at least one hour.

PART 2

1. Preheat oven to 350°F.
2. For each candy cane, shape 1 teaspoon dough of each color into 4 to 6-inch rope.
3. For smooth, even strips, roll back and forth on lightly floured board.
4. Place 1 red and 1 white strip side by side; press together lightly and twist.
5. Place on ungreased cookie sheet.
6. Curve top down to form handle of cane.
7. Bake until set and very light brown, about 7 to 9 minutes.
8. Mix candy and granulated sugar; immediately sprinkle over cookies.
9. Allow cookies to cool completely before removing from cookie sheet.

If you have enjoyed this book or
it has touched your life in some way,
we would love to hear from you.

Please send your comments to:
Hallmark Book Feedback
P.O. Box 419034
Mail Drop 215
Kansas City, MO 64141

Or e-mail us at:
booknotes@hallmark.com